Mike McGrath's
Book of Compost

D0028955

Mike McGrath's Book of Compost

Mike McGrath

Host of Public Radio's *You Bet Your Garden*

Illustrated by Signe Wilkinson
Winner of the Pulitzer Prize
in Editorial Cartooning

Sterling Publishing Co., Inc.
New York

Library of Congress Cataloging-in-Publication Data Available

10 9 8 7 6 5 4 3 2 1

Published by Sterling Publishing Co., Inc.
387 Park Avenue South, New York, NY 10016
Text © 2006 by Mike McGrath
Illustrations © 2006 by Signe Wilkinson
Distributed in Canada by Sterling Publishing
c/o Canadian Manda Group, 165 Dufferin Street
Toronto, Ontario, Canada M6K 3H6
Distributed in the United Kingdom by GMC Distribution Services
Castle Place, 166 High Street, Lewes, East Sussex, England BN7 1XU
Distributed in Australia by Capricorn Link (Australia) Pty. Ltd.
P.O. Box 704, Windsor, NSW 2756, Australia

Manufactured in the United States of America
All rights reserved

Designed by Carol Petro

Sterling ISBN-13: 978-1-4027-3398-7
        ISBN-10: 1-4027-3398-4

For information about custom editions, special sales, premium and
corporate purchases, please contact Sterling Special Sales
Department at 800-805-5489 or specialsales@sterlingpub.com.

*This book is dedicated to Sir Albert Howard
and J. I. Rodale, who together brought the
science of composting to America; to the many
researchers and home composting enthusiasts
who have helped define and refine the technique;
to Mother Nature and her millions of miniscule
minions who masterfully motivate this matchless
metamorphic miracle; to my wonderful editor,
Hannah Reich, who meritoriously managed to
make this missive materialize; and to Clover,
the Garden Fairy, who watches over all
composters, big and small.*

—Mike McG, 2006

Contents

 # Introduction

Hi! I'm Mike McGrath, your host for this tour of "The Wonderful World of Composting." What's that? Why *ME?* What do *I* know about this, you ask? (Don't deny it—I heard you! These books work both ways, you know!)

Anyway, these are fair questions. There are a lot of people out there making grand pronouncements about this subject who never actually turned a single maple leaf into food for their fennel. That's *not* the case with *moi*, however.

I learned quite a bit about the nature and science of composting during my seven years as editor-in-chief of *Organic Gardening* magazine. And I have continued to study this fascinating subject so that I can provide the best possible answers and up-to-date info to the listeners of my nationally syndicated Public Radio show, **You Bet Your Garden,** when they call in with composting questions, which those wonderful listeners do with great regularity.

But perhaps most important, I have been *personally* composting for over 20 years—everything from:

* Tossing lots of stuff into big piles

* Containing carefully measured ingredients in bins

* Using every possible type of spinner, tumbler, and other device in my own personal Compost Corral—where I create all the black gold my many gardens rely upon.

So sit back and relax as I walk us through the reasons we compost, the wonders the end result can achieve in your garden and landscape, and exactly how to do it.

In which we explain why you should make your own black gold, what you should include in your mix of raw ingredients, what you should leave out, and why you should never, ever leave out leaves.

☀ An Imitation of Nature

I want to start by giving you four gifts: Free plant-feeding fertilizer, free weed-preventing mulch, free clay- and sandy-soil improver, and free plant-disease prevention. And I can fit all four inside one package, because they're what you receive when you apply compost to your lawn and garden.

Two to four inches a year of compost (depending on your location—we'll explain in a bit) will feed every single one of your outdoor—and indoor—plants; and it will feed them better than any chemical fertilizer (and better than just about any packaged organic one, too)!

Compost suppresses weeds and keeps moisture in the soil as well or better than wood chips, so-called "premium triple-shredded bark," dyed wood, or other mulches—and it does so without the risk of killing your plants and irrevocably staining your home and car. Compost actually improves your soil structure—even when you just spread it on top of your lawn. And compost fights plant diseases—including the dreaded black spot on roses—better than any chemical fungicide. Now that's a gift— eh, make that "gifts"—that keeps on giving.

If *your* landscape has been looking a little blah lately, maybe it's because your trees and shrubs are hungry. Or *hung over*—from the hard hit those poor plants take when you hose them down with the concentrated salts in chemical fertilizers like Osmocote and Miracle-Gro.

Maybe your lawn is equally fat or famished—or maybe its soil has become heavy and compacted from years of foot traffic. Perhaps under- or over-feeding has made your garden plants poor performers and easy targets for pests and disease.

It really doesn't matter exactly what *your* specific problem is—because compost is the answer to virtually every garden question.

Compost provides the *perfect* amount of food for every plant—including essential nutrients not found in commercial fertilizers. Raking compost into your turf improves the structure of the soil *under* your lawn. **And** it increases your plants' ability to fend off foes without any help from you! Whew—I'm exhausted just thinking about it!

OK—now, let's be honest; I know that a lot of you out there cringe a little bit when the subject of composting comes up. After all, if you've been gardening out of boxes and bottles with big warning labels on them all your life, turning to a mixture of leaves and last night's leftovers probably seems a little strange. But composting is simply our way of imitating how Nature feeds Herself: Nobody spread chemical fertilizers on the Great Plains, the biggest, most beautiful lawn of all. No one had to spray fungicides on America's vast fields of wildflowers to protect them from disease. And the magnificent forests of this nation grew tall without anyone applying pesticides to those trees.

That's right—if you think that plants need chemicals to survive, just look around! The woods, plains, and wildflowers sustain themselves without any man-made materials.

The roots of trees reach deep down into the earth, pulling up minerals and nutrients from far deeper than most plants can reach. Sure, they use some of this food. But much remains in their leaves, which feed the plants on the ground when they fall.

Summer weeds, grasses, and wildflowers killed by frost return *their* nutrients to the soil. And of course, deer, birds, squirrels, and other animals make daily "contributions" and then release a huge store of nutrients when they die. The greatest "gardens" the world has ever seen have been nurtured for untold centuries by this seemingly impossible perpetual motion machine that uses living and dying plants to power untold generations of future plants, a surprisingly simple process whose astonishing power we harness when we make compost.

2 The Overwhelming Importance of Fall Leaves

S imply put, nothing improves the health of a garden better than adding organic matter to your soil; and composting the natural materials that collect in your household allows you to do just that without making a single trip to a store or having anything delivered. But it is Fall leaves that make it all happen.

As we'll explain in more detail as we proceed, the best compost is made by mixing smallish amounts of nitrogen-rich materials like your kitchen scraps, spent garden plants, and lawn clippings with large amounts of "dry brown" carbon-rich stuff. And the very best material for the dry brown part of this equation is Fall leaves. They are the perfect match for the wet green matter you'll be recycling, and they are *filled* with trace minerals and nutrients the tree's roots have extracted from deep in the earth, minerals and trace nutrients essential for plant health, but completely missing from commercial chemical fertilizers (and totally tapped out in most garden and farm soils).

It all starts with you shredding up those leaves. And, yes, shred you must! *Whole* leaves take *quite* a while to break down on their own, and tend to mat together, creating a darn good imitation of a tarp. Whole leaves just sit there cold in compost piles. Not only don't they help—they can actually *PREVENT* the composting process.

Shred them up, however, and you create the ***perfect*** compost makings. (Got *lots* of trees? Shredded leaves also make a perfect weed-suppressing garden mulch!) My favorite way to shred leaves is with a leaf blower. Yes, most people *DO* just use these machines to blow their leaves onto the *neighbor's* lawn and driveway, making them perhaps the most appropriately named piece of outdoor power equipment.

But most blowers have a reverse setting and attachments that allow you to suck those leaves up into a shoulder bag or other

container. *AND* all of the machines that *DO* have this reverse setting also have a built-in shredder that minces those leaves perfectly (into "mince-leaf"?) as you collect them. You suck them up whole and they go into the bag in shreds. So, instead of you and your neighbor endlessly blowing the same leaves back and forth onto each other's driveways all Fall, you do the job *ONCE*; sucking them up and shredding them all at the very same time.

Now, as we said, this shredding *is* very important to your composting success.

But something else is happening that's equally important. As those leaves get shredded, their volume decreases greatly. This is what it means when a blower/vac's packaging or advertising cites a "mulching ratio" of 10 to 1 or 12 to 1 or even 20 to 1. And those *ARE* the numbers that are achieved: Shredding leaves generally reduces their volume by *at least* a factor of ten. In other words, you should be able to empty ten bags jammed full of whole leaves onto the ground, suck them up with a blower/vac and then fit those shredded leaves back into just one of those bags.

This means two things. One is that you're concentrating a *lot* more plant energy and nutrition into your bins, spinners, or drums when you fill them with shreds instead of "wholes." The other is the simple fact that you'll be able to store ten bags' worth of whole leaves in just one bag! No more excuses about not having enough space—I just increased your storage capacity by a factor of ten!

Don't forget—leaves "Fall" just once a year, but you're generating green waste from your kitchen and from other nitrogen-rich matter that you'll want to recycle all season long. When Fall is upon us, don't just consider the compost you'll make then and there: Think about the future—Winter, Spring, Summer. You want to make sure you'll have enough leaves on hand to mix with your kitchen waste all the way through to *NEXT* Fall.

I speak from unhappy experience here. I *used* to bag up whole leaves and then shred them up whenever I needed to put more stuff in my piles. But no matter how many bags I filled each Fall, I always ran out *early* in the Summer (sometimes as early in the Summer as mid-Spring), which is a HUGE bummer! As we'll discuss in more detail in a bit, Fall leaves are very difficult to replace in the composting process. For instance, broken-up straw bales—probably the best alternative to leaves—are OK; at least they provide the dry brown bulk needed to balance your wet greens. But they're heavy and dirty to work with, difficult to shred, don't contain anywhere *near* the concentrated plant nutrition of Fall leaves *AND* you have to *BUY* those bales. The (vastly superior) leaves are free!

Honestly, none of your "dry brown" alternatives are anywhere near as rich in trace minerals and other nutrients as leaves. And I can almost guarantee that your garden plants are craving those minerals; they're the first thing that gets exhausted in our soil! So I learned my lesson (the hard way, as usual; I know you feel my pain) and now I shred *EVERY* single leaf right away. And guess what I learned? Just ten bags of those concentrated cuties (which would have taken up a whopping 120 to 150 bags when whole) is enough to take me all the way through the year—and without needing a leaf storage area that's as big as my house!

So quit blowing and start sucking!

Be ready to capture all the leaves you possibly can—and don't be shy: Tell your neighbors that you'll be happy to take *their* leaves if they're foolish enough to throw those valuable treasures away!

And although I have found it to be the hands-down absolute best way to achieve shredded-leaf nirvana, you don't *HAVE* to use a leaf blower set on reverse. You can also shred them with the "shredder" portion of a chipper/shredder, a dedicated "leaf shredder" machine, a lawnmower, a string trimmer in a leaf-filled trashcan (be very careful if you go this route; heavy gloves and safety goggles are an absolute *MUST!*), or just rake them into a big pile and warn lots of kids not to jump up and down on them for three hours.

And if you're one of those folks who really *does* want to make your own compost, but you're not quite sure what should go into it, and/or you fear attracting pests and such, just start with Fall leaves—and *end* with them, too.

That's right, if you're worried that you'll include the wrong things or attract strange creatures of the night, just compost your shredded leaves alone! Fall leaves are one of the two things (barnyard manures are the other) that you can successfully compost all by themselves. All you need to do is shred them up and they'll *quickly* transform into rich, black super-soil. The French have been relying on this mineral-rich leaf mold (or horticultural mold) to feed *their* plants for centuries: "*Le moule horticole*" or *"moule de feuille." Il est magnifique!*

Compost Ingredient Do's and Don'ts— Grass-Clipping Couture

As we just said, you can compost shredded leaves all by their lonesome and get really good compost. But the *BEST* "black gold" is made by mixing those "dry brown" carbon-rich leaves with what we call "wet green" nitrogen-rich materials. And *this* is where we lose a lot of people. They just want to make compost and all of a

THE RICH, BLACK COMPOST NICELY SETS OFF MY PETALS DON'T YOU THINK?

SHE'D BE NOTHING WITHOUT ME!

sudden the sources they're consulting are talking about achieving things like a "30-to-1 carbon-to-nitrogen ratio." Now, that *IS* the ideal mixture, but that number doesn't mean anything to an ordinary gardener who has no real way of judging the relative carbon and nitrogen content of their raw materials.

(Note: This is the spot in other composting books where you'd normally see a chart listing the relative carbon-to-nitrogen ratios of common compost ingredients. Well, guess what?—We're NOT going to do it! Because you don't *need* no stinkin' chart!)

I often fear that the possibility of this simple process suddenly involving complex math scares a lot of people away. So relax—I can assure you that I have *never* once attempted to figure out a carbon-to-nitrogen ratio and have cooked up hundreds of batches of fabulous black gold over the years. Generally speaking, combining about four parts of shredded leaves to one part of "wet green" nitrogen-rich material, by volume, makes the best compost.

And as long as you remember that it's the Fall leaves that are The Bee's Knees here, you have a *lot* of wiggle room inside that huge generality. The important thing to remember is the *purpose* each of those two basic kinds of ingredients serves. We could fill up a book ten times this size with the details of what goes on inside a cooking pile—and we *will* briefly discuss the amazing changes that take place in there a little later on. But for now, my favorite simple explanation is that the dry brown shredded leaves come into the picture teeming with microbes; the wet green, nitrogen-rich material is food for those microbes. When they get together, things get hot, and you get compost.

Now, one of the easiest ways to make this kind of combo-compost is with your lawn mower. Just give your grass a cutting when it's covered with Fall leaves, collect that perfect combination of well-shredded and completely mixed brown and very-nitrogen-rich green material as you go, and then empty your collection bags into a big wire bin, tumbler, or similar structure. It'll start cooking down into rich, black super-soil right away; you may even see steam rising from that pile the next morning.

Now come the cautions.

If you use chemical herbicides on your lawn:

1. **Shame on you!** Those herbicides are a huge threat to your health, and the health of your family, pets, and the environment.

2. You *can* still use the compost that results, but *only* on that lawn itself—it could harm other plants. That's right—some of the herbicides used on American lawns are so toxic and so persistent that they survive even the hottest compost piles; and the compost that results could wipe out a garden, shrubs, even trees.

And the worst part of all this is that those chemical herbicides were totally unnecessary. If you grow the right grass for your region and cut it at the correct height (two to three and a half inches tall* AFTER you're done cutting) you'll never *see* a weed!

Let's discuss those grass clippings a little further. *VERY* high in nitrogen—10 percent by weight—they are great components in a pile. And the Fall mowing method we just described is the ideal way to incorporate them. But grass clippings *ALONE* are a very bad idea. I want to stress that you can *NOT* compost *any* green material like grass clippings or your kitchen waste alone under *any* circumstances. You'll get a garbage dump, not a compost pile.

Shredded leaves all by themselves? Fine—you'll get really good compost.

Grass clippings all alone? *Yuck!*

Kitchen waste all alone? *Double* yuck!

(Hey—one more "yuck" and we've got Curly from *The Three Stooges!*)

A big heap of kitchen waste or grass clippings will just sit there, looking and smelling *very* bad. But mixing small amounts of those very same kitchen scraps in with large amounts of shredded leaves will

---

* Two inches for warm-season grasses (Bermuda and others typically grown down South), three inches for Kentucky blue and other cool-season (i.e. Northern) grasses in sun, and a three-and-a-half-inch cut for fescues and other cool-season turfs growing in shade.

make compost nicely. No mess, no smell—even if it's just all in a big pile sitting out in the open.

You'll notice I specified *kitchen waste* just then. Fresh grass clippings are a little trickier—they have a tendency to mat together into a sticky mass that resists composting. And besides—one of the best ways to feed your lawn is to return all the nitrogen in those clips to the soil by using a mulching mower. If you divert a lot of those clippings to the compost pile, you'll have to feed the lawn that much more. It makes a lot more sense to obtain a high-quality mulching mower, keep the blades razor sharp and let the pulverized, dust-like mulched clippings go back to the earth right then and there. (*REAL* mulching mowers grind those clips to dust; you don't see visible "clippings" on the lawn afterward.)

But if you have an *excess* of herbicide-free clips, you should certainly incorporate them into your pile. Let them dry for a day or two first and then mix them into your bin or pile slowly, and in small amounts. Don't just toss huge handfuls in!

…*Unless* you're using a closed system that makes your compost easy to turn, like a spinner or tumbler; then you can simply allow that built-in turning mechanism to mix those clips in when you give the drums their daily spin. Otherwise, you *must* stop and mix those clippings up completely with shredded leaves BEFORE you put them in your bin.

OK? Now let's get to what you've been waiting for—let's talk garbage!

4 Kitchen "*Gabige*" Do's and Don'ts—Turning Your Trash Into Garden Gold!

R ecycling your kitchen waste is one of the big reasons people love making their own compost—especially if you're like me and fret over every bit of wasted food.

Composting *greatly* eases your conscience; that leftover food isn't wasted—its inherent energy is going into growing next year's garden (instead of growing a landfill—or, come to think of it, growing *YOU*). Recycling enthusiasts are especially keen on the idea; they're amazed at how much waste—teeming with unused nutrients—they're able to divert from their "trash." And the trash they *DO* put out is much drier and a lot less sloppy—all the "slop" (as my Grandmom Elsie used to call non-dry kitchen trash) is going into the compost!

So: *EXACTLY* what's in and what's out?

Included in your compost bucket should be all your vegetable waste—those browned lettuce leaves, uneaten apple cores, trimmed-off roots and stuff. Big items, like tough, fibrous broccoli stalks, should be chopped up first to hasten their decomposition. And whole fruits that have gone bad should at least be quartered—unless you want to see that ugly orange poking up out of your pile two months later. You should also include all your used tea bags and coffee grounds.

Yes, coffee grounds. They're **GREAT**—one of the richest sources of plant-feeding, compost-heating nitrogen your kitchen can supply. Go ahead and include the paper filters as well—they'll break down nicely.

Eggshells are also a BIG yes; your plants will *looove* getting their calcium—most garden soils are deficient in this essential plant nutrient, which prevents blossom-end rot in tomatoes, improves the health of many other garden plants, and makes all your veggie garden members taste better! Just air dry and then crush those shells up first to make sure they break down completely.

And these two super-premium compost components don't have to come exclusively from *YOUR* household. If you don't eat a lot of eggs, ask some of your friends who do indulge to save their shells for you. (It's definitely worth it—just wait'll you see what the calcium those shells impart to your finished compost does for the health of your plants.) Same with coffee; if you're not a "drinker," bring home the used grounds from your coffee corner at work, or ask the local java hut to save some grounds for you. Starbucks even has a program where they provide gardeners with five-pound bags of their nitrogen-rich grounds; ask about the "Grounds for Gardeners" program at your local Starbucks.

But *no* egg *insides.* And **no meat, bones, fat, dairy, or other animal products.** With one big exception: If you are composting inside a high-quality *closed* unit, you CAN include lobster, crab and shrimp shells. These are *POWERFULLY* rich in nitrogen and will really get your compost cooking *HOT*—which you want. *And* those shells contain important trace elements and hard-to-find nutrients that can really benefit plants—especially down South, where the resulting compost might well have the power to chase away the destructive root knot nematodes that so pester warm-weather growers, thanks to the chitin content of those shells.

But because they *ARE* so nitrogen rich, don't overdo it; no more than say, a gallon of shells in a standard bin or tumbler chamber. Make sure you've got plenty of shredded leaves in there to help them cook down, and chop them up into small pieces first.

Same with fish debris—small amounts can be very good *IF* they're well chopped up first *and* you're composting inside a closed unit. Don't add seafood parts to an open pile, exposed bin, or even a sealed plastic unit; it will quickly turn into a raccoon buffet. (And don't even add them to a high-quality closed metal unit if you have bears roaming free in your area; they'll rip your composter into little bitty pieces to get at those treats.)

Other good green materials include all of your spent-but-healthy garden plants. (Throw obviously diseased plants in the trash instead.) And, yes, you *can* include weeds—*IF* they have not yet gone to seed. And you *should* include them, especially dandelions and other weeds with long taproots. Those roots are rich in minerals that your garden plants will *looove* to get. (I let my pulled dandelions dry in the sun for a while before I chop them up and put them into my piles—again, just to be safe.)

No ashes from barbecue grills or coal fires. And *no* dog or cat poop—*ever, ever, EVER*. Even pets that are *always* kept indoors can harbor dangerous parasites found in meat-eating animals.

But the poop and bedding of *herbivores*—pets that *don't* ever eat meat—like rabbits, gerbils, and guinea pigs, are great to include. So is llama poop if you happen to have the opportunity, and I personally never visit the zoo or circus without seeing if there's any elephant or rhino poop to spare. But "no" to the big cat stuff—no matter what you've heard about it repelling deer—as they are essentially just big kitty cats. (With paws the size of your head and teeth like giant daggers. "Oh—isn't he cute? Here kitty, kitty...**Aiiiiyyy!**")

"Barnyard manures" are great to include if you have access—especially horse manure, which is fairly "hot" (nitrogen-rich), and poultry manure, which is *VERY* hot and *super*-nitrogen rich. Either of those will help your pile heat up quickly. And since "manure" by definition always comes with bedding (usually straw or wood shavings), it already has an ideal carbon-to-nitrogen ratio. That's why it's the other thing you can compost "alone" and get great results—thanks to that dry brown bedding material.

And, finally, it's always a good idea to toss in a handful of finished compost every time you mix up a fresh batch of raw ingredients that you hope to turn into compost. If you don't have any finished compost, toss in a couple of handfuls of your best garden soil.

On the scientific side, this little addition will "inoculate" your compost-to-be with lots of the wonderful microorganisms that make it all happen. And on the pure *gardening* side, such a thing is good luck. And, as we gardeners know *all* too well, we *need* that luck more than normal people.

(Note: No matter what it says on the box, *don't* add commercial compost starters or activators at this point; I'll reveal a bit later in the book when these things can be much more useful.)

☀ 5 Let's Make Some Black Gold!

All right—now you know *why* we're doing it, and *what* (and what not) to include. Now it's time to delve into the how. So let's get dirty with the details, beginning with the difference between hot and cold composting.

"*Cold*" is a synonym for anaerobic composting; that is, "without oxygen." This is the classic "pile it all up somewhere and it will eventually rot" scenario. And it *will*. Farmers have been making free fertilizer for themselves by combining their mixed field waste and stable sweepings in "mulch piles" for centuries. Which brings us to one of the most interesting facts about composting—the larger the amount of raw material you stack up, the hotter the center will become, even if the ingredients are *way* out of proportion, brown- and green-wise.

And so, because of their sheer volume—often the size of a double-wide or larger—some of these farm piles heat up *brilliantly* (and often surprisingly to the mulch*er*), many pouring vast amounts of steam out their tops and drawing the attention of the local fire department.

One large-scale composting enthusiast in California garnered a ton of national publicity years ago when he created a farmer-size pile by entreating everyone in the area to contribute their yard waste. Thanks to its eventual enormous volume—and a very high proportion of dried grass clippings—it began to steam mightily and was eventually torn apart and hauled away by fearful local authorities. ("Look out—she's gonna blow!")

Such piles are very exciting. But the common household pile is just the opposite. Much smaller in size—generally *way* too small to achieve that wonderful internal combustion—it's the dullard of the party that just seems to *sit* there *forever.*

But then, when you get disgusted by its seeming inaction and tear it apart, you find—hidden behind layers of uncomposted material you have been looking at for MUCH too long—some amount of *FINE*-looking compost, nice and rich and black and earthy, generally at the very bottom and center of the pile.

Yes, you *can* use that compost. But it is vastly inferior stuff (see the details below). Besides, we are preaching the gospel of **hot** compost in this book!

HOT compost—yessir! Hot-cha-cha-cha! *Super* compost! Compost that can leap tall cornstalks in a single bound! Bend zucchini in its bare hands! And who, disguised as….

Anyway, cold compost would also make for a *REALLY* short book. ("Pile it all up and if it's at least half leaves it'll eventually turn into compost. The End." You asleep yet, kids?)

Yes, a reasonably well-assembled smallish mass of stuff just sitting out in a pile will eventually rot. (So will a poorly assembled small mass, but you wouldn't want to smell and/or look at it for long, much less years.)

In Nature, *every* living thing eventually rots (as those of us pushing certain numbers realize all too well), and so cold piles *do* eventually yield composts of varying quality. When the typical homeowner does this without the aid of barnyard manures, the process generally takes several years and yields a fairly low-quality compost. It *will* improve soil structure nicely, and it is an OK plant food. But it has no power to prevent and cure plant disease and should not be used to make compost tea (subjects we'll discuss at length in a bit).

Big, open piles rarely look anything other than unattractive, as well; which is fine out on the farm, but pretty rude—and in many cases, illegal—in the city.

That's why people started using bins to contain their cooking compost, giving it structure, holding it more upright and moving things along much faster. For me, the classic design will always be the "Lehigh-style wooden bin," advocated by the original editor and founder of *Organic Gardening* magazine, the great J. I. Rodale.

Named for either the Pennsylvania county or university where it was developed (or both), the Lehigh bin is a box-shaped, four by four by four–foot design made up of a series of cedar wood slats joined at the four corners by long metal rods. The slats are stacked so that there's an open space the size of a slat between each of them, allowing oxygen to reach all the outside portions while still containing the ingredients nicely.

They're very easy to build if you're at all handy, and can often be purchased ready-made online and in better garden centers.

If such a pile is turned once or twice over its composting life—moving the stuff that was on the outside to the center and vice-versa—you will create a nicely aerobic (well-oxygenated) pile that will quickly cook up a high-quality compost with increased plant nutrition capabilities and great potential to prevent and cure plant diseases.

Here's the easiest path to turning a Lehigh heap:

* Assemble your pile; filling the bin all the way to the top with the right mixture of well-shredded dry browns (lots) and chopped-up wet greens (not-so-lots).

* Wait a week in warm weather, a month in cool.

✳ Lift the wooden bin structure up; it should come away from the (now-somewhat-smaller) cube of composting material easily. Place the structure nearby and then shovel or fork the contents back in, trying to move the stuff that *was* in the center to the outside and the stuff that *was* on the outside to the middle.

✳ A week (or month) later, do it again.

Now you're cookin'!

Variations on this theme include bins made of heavy-gauge animal fencing. They don't look nearly as nice, but are much less expensive, can be made any size (again, the bigger the better), and have better airflow. Their contents will still need to be turned once or twice to get that center portion some air exposure and to expose the outside to the heat that's generated only in the center of a pile...

...UNLESS you put a **chimney** in the middle, that is. **Here's my absolute best composting trick:**

Roll some of that animal fencing into hollow tubes the diameter of your arm or leg, and stick a rolled tube into the center of each pile *before* you start adding the raw ingredients, making sure the top of the tube extends above the top of the bin or cage. Then assemble your raw ingredients (well mixed and shredded, of course) around the outside of this chimney, so that the chimney stays nice and upright in the middle, with as little of your raw material as possible falling inside. (A larger-diameter chimney takes up more room, but is much easier to reach down inside and keep clean. The less stuff you leave inside that chimney, the more air it will draw to the center of your pile.)

The chimney acts as a powerful aerator, pulling oxygen to the center of the pile, greatly speeding the transformation to Garden Gold. And I do mean *powerful!* Here's a great way to see the difference for yourself: When Fall arrives, make two big compost corrals out of animal fencing; make them exactly the same size. Assemble your shredded leaves and other ingredients and fill one corral up with a chimney in the middle and one without. Then come out early the next morning—I'll bet you see steam and heat waves rising out of that chimney. But that's not the best. Hold your hand over the top of the chimney—you'll be startled by the rush of warm air rising up. The pile with the chimney will be done faster, and its compost will be a much better quality than the one without.

Is a chimney as good as a few turns of the ingredients? Maybe. Is a pile that's "chimnied" *AND* turned The Bee's Knees? You betcha!

Big Tip! I grow a lot of tomatoes (or as we correctly pronounce them in my native Phil-Elf-ya: "tamatas"); big, rangy heirloom varieties that require large cages made of animal fencing to contain them. Those cages ensure that I'll harvest the maximum number and highest quality fruits, but they can also be a real chore to store. Ah—but they come out of service at the end of the gardening season, just before the Fall leaves come tumbling down!

So instead of unrolling them and getting my poor hands all chewed up ("**Gloves?!** Do I *LOOK* like a wuss??!!"), I remove the spent vines and fill those cages; some get filled with big batches of raw ingredients to compost down and the rest get filled with just plain shredded Fall leaves.

By the time I need those cages again (around June 1st—I'm both a slight coward and compassionate enough to realize that tomatoes don't enjoy cool nights *and* that I'll still get my first ripe tomato on the same day as if I had put them out in May and coddled them along), the compost-filled ones are...well, filled with compost! The leaf-filled ones are leaf-mold compost on the bottom and shredded leaves perfect for mulching on the top.

An alternative open-air configuration is the **three-bin system**. This consists of a large structure (with or without a roof; *with* where there's too much rain; *without* where there's often too little) composed of three chambers with slatted side openings for airflow (much like the Lehigh bin). You put raw materials into the first section until it's all filled up. When ya can't add no more, you use a pitchfork (or in large systems, a front-end loader) to move this somewhat-breaking-down material into the middle bin so that you can once again use the first one for really raw materials.

When that first section is again filled up, you move the middle-chamber material over to the third chamber and the first-chamber material into the now-vacant middle. When you've filled up the first chamber for the third time, the material in the third chamber should be completely composted—thanks to all the mixing and turning it has received while on the move. If you're looking to get some more physical activity into your life and/or you generate a *lot* of organic waste, the three-bin system is for you.

But the dirty little secret of organic gardening is that very few people *do* turn their compost, and many piles that were *intended* to produce hot, aerobic, disease-fighting black gold in a month or so instead are left to sit, finally becoming cold, anaerobic compost a year or three later. That's one of the reasons why tumblers, spinners, and drums were invented. These devices are designed with the mixing of the contents in mind.

With *spinners*—essentially giant trash cans fastened up high on a metal stand—*you* provide all the power, turning the whole schmageggie hiney-over-teakettle a couple of times by grabbing hold of a handle and giving it the kind of spin that would use up the whole half hour on *Wheel of Fortune*. These are often made by taking giant heavy plastic barrels that were originally used for bulk shipments of olives and attaching a spindle to them.

Drum composters utilize the science of leverage to help those of us who are no longer going out of our way to seek out heavy lifting and yet wish to make our compost quickly. You turn a crank and a gear system uses that energy to turn a big drum—theoretically with less effort on your part than if you had just manhandled the thing.

Drums and spinners are batch composters. That is, you open the thing up, fill it *completely* with the correct mix of dry browns and wet greens, close it up, and then use the handle or crank or whatever to mix things up every day. If your device has nice, big, screened ventilation holes and you started with the right raw ingredients—especially if some of your nitrogen is hot, like coffee grounds, seafood shells, or barnyard manures—you could have finished compost in as little as two weeks.

But because the ingredients in any system shrink down to half their size during the composting process, people are tempted to keep adding stuff. That's why we always tell people to have a second pile or tumbler handy; once you fill up one, you need to let it compost 'til it's finished. New raw ingredients should be saved up or placed in another bin or tumbler. (One premium tumbler—the "ComposTwin"—has dual chambers that make it easy to batch; you use one side for tossing in raw stuff and one side for cooking compost).

There are also closed composting units that just sit there. The "Earth Machine" is one of the classics—it's a big, round, black plastic unit with a removable cover on top for adding raw ingredients and a removable coal-chute-like door at the bottom for harvesting finished compost. (Remember—no matter what system you use, the stuff on the bottom will always be ready first.)

It actually works better than it sounds—especially if you treat it like a batch composter, filling it all the way to the top and then just letting it sit (preferably in part sun) 'til it's done. If you *MUST* continue adding raw ingredients to the top as it cooks down, make sure you have a big pile of shredded leaves handy to mix in with the garbage you're recycling. If you get good at figuring out the timing of the cooking inside such a unit, you could keep adding a nice mixture of brown and green to the top and regularly remove finished compost from the bottom.

Or, if you have the room, have several on hand and use them in sequence. The Earth Machine is one of the units that local municipalities and extension offices purchase in bulk and give away (or sell for a nominal fee—usually $10) to folks who take a composting class. I've seen demonstration areas where half a dozen are lined up in a row, and they look cute as all heck.

Yes, this is "cold composting," and yes, we do prefers our hot compost, yes we does. But if this is all you can do, it can work very well to provide you with a perfectly adequate plant food and soil improver. And if you want to use such a device to make *hot* compost for fighting plant disease, simply lift the whole thing up, move it over to the side, and fork the ingredients back into the unit in its new location a couple of times during the composting process—just like we suggested for the Lehigh bin a little while back.

Or get yourself a "compost aerator." This cool tool looks a little like a miniature pogo stick. You hold the handle, shove the rest of the spike-like device into your pile, and pull it back up toward you. When you do, "wings" open up on the bottom of the device and move the contents of your pile around. Plunge and then pull. Move to a different spot in the pile, plunge, and pull. Move again, plunge again, and pull again. It's not as good as moving your pile "next door," but it is a *lot* better than letting it just sit there. Plunging your pile a few times a week will really help speed things up. These devices cost about $20-$30, and there are several styles widely available. You can find aerators at your local garden supply store or online. (Type "compost aerator" to search online.)

Anyway, sealed units are perfect for folks who live near other houses and want to make some compost but are worried about the neighbors' reactions to open piles. Some even have cleverly arranged holes or slits to allow rainwater to percolate in and keep the ingredients moist. Which brings us to…

A word about moisture. Here where I compost, in Pennsylvania, we get enough rain that I rarely have to worry about my open piles and bins drying out. In fact, some years when it never seems to *STOP* raining, I'll cover those open piles with a big tarp during downpours.

But if you live in a dry region—or you're composting inside a closed unit—you'll want to make sure your compost doesn't dry out. Have a hose handy when you assemble your raw ingredients, and moisten your shredded leaves as you mix them in.

You don't have to really soak them—unless your "wet green" materials aren't all that wet.

Then check your compost-to-be every other week or so. If it seems dry, give it a little watering. Again, don't worry too much about exact amounts—this is *COOKING*, not *BAKING*, and you have a lot of wiggle room. Basically, your goal is for both the raw ingredients and your finished compost to have the consistency of a wrung-out, but damp sponge. Not bone dry, not soaking wet; in the middle is just right.

And if the Goldilocks method doesn't work for you, purchase a moisture meter—you can get these inexpensive electrical probe devices online and at most garden centers. They're great to have around if you have lots of houseplants—you won't be guessing as to whether they need water or not.

(NOTE: If you live in a *legendary* hot and dry region [Arizona comes to mind], you might want to investigate "pit composting." Rather than sitting aboveground, your raw ingredients rest in a pit, covered with straw or palm fronds or some other such material to retain as much moisture as possible. Contact your local county extension office for details and plans.)

So—when is your black gold *finished*?

What *should* happen to a correctly made hot batch is that it will quickly start cooking, as all those bacteria and other microorganisms get to know each other better. The center of a perfectly made pile will heat up to as much as 160 degrees—creating compost in the shortest amount of time possible *AND* killing off weed seeds and disease spores. If you want to monitor this amazing process, get a compost thermometer—these inexpensive devices look like big meat thermometers; you just push the long stake into the center of the pile and it'll tell you how hot that center gets. Very neat! You'll find them for sale in most garden catalogs and at better garden centers.

(An enthusiast in California used to demonstrate the thermic potential of a well-made pile every Thanksgiving by piling up really quick-cooking raw materials and then placing a raw turkey in a roasting pan—sealed with duct tape—in the center. Twenty-four hours later, the turkey was perfectly done. Note: Kids! This man is a professional—don't try this at home.)

Check that pile every day if you *do* decide to use a thermometer, because compost that heats up quickly will also cool back down after a few days—so don't miss it. After it cools completely, and the contents have been reduced in volume by a third to a half, it's ready to check for doneness.

Take some out and hold it in your hands: Does it have that wet-sponge consistency? Is it dark and rich-looking? Does it have a nice earthy odor, but no objectionable smells? If you said yes to all of those, it's ready to go!

But what if it's not??!

We'll cover all the possible problems you may encounter in the chapters that follow.

In which we explain how you're going to employ the wonderful material you have now created to improve the structure of your soil, feed and mulch your plants, and give nasty horticultural diseases the bum's rush.

Compost as Basic Plant Food and Soil Improver

Back in our last thrilling episode, we discussed what ingredients to include in your compost-to-be, the best ways to contain those raw ingredients, and how to make the highest-quality compost out of them. This time around, we'll discuss exactly how best to use that black gold to perk up your plants perfectly!

Now, as we mentioned just a few short sentences ago (OK—but it *WOULD* be true if I knew *how* to write short sentences), your compost is ready to use when it looks like rich, black super-soil and smells nice and earthy.

SCREENING COMPOST

We also always used to say, "and when you can't recognize any of the original ingredients," but the truth is that you're almost always going to see the occasional half an orange or a couple of wood chips in even the finest compost—along with funny-to-embarrassing items that fell into the garbage container while it was still in the kitchen, like knives, forks, and Star Wars action figures. (Jabba the Hut! What a relief—I thought you were a big ugly slug! Actually, come to think of it, you *ARE* just a big…)

You have three options when you notice that a batch of finished compost still contains small amounts of the odd original ingredient here and there.

1. Pick that stuff out by hand and toss the unfinished material into your next batch.

2. Just ignore it and use the compost as is, especially if you're mixing it into your soil. That stuff will continue to decompose down in the earth. But *don't* go this route if there's a fair amount of *woody* material present; such a batch needs to be recomposted or cleaned up thoroughly. Screening it would be ideal. Which brings us to:

3. Screen it out.

Screening is a great extra step that ensures you'll be using only premium-grade compost—and it's essential when you want to use your home-made compost in a potting mixture. It's easy to make a screen out of hardware cloth—a material that's a lot like window screening, but made of heavy-duty metal, with larger openings than on regular screening; you'll find it for sale in rolls at larger home centers and hardware stores. Just cut a piece of this metal "cloth" to the desired shape with a pair of tin snips and attach it to a wooden frame—ideally one that fits nicely over the top of your wheelbarrow.

Then, whenever you want to separate out the very best of your black gold, take some big handfuls of supposedly finished compost and roll and rub it across the screening. Compost that's nicely fine but temporarily clumped will be broken up and will fall on through. But chunks of *truly* unfinished material will remain on top.

Whatever goes down easily into the barrow is ready to use; anything that doesn't get through can be used in a less important situation—like to feed trees or shrubs—or tossed into the next pile to finish composting.

If you don't want to make your own screen, you can buy one. Many garden catalogs and hardware stores carry compost screens in a variety of sizes. They may call them soil sifters or soil screens or sifting screens or something similar instead of using the word "compost" in the name.

Screened compost will *definitely* be "finished." And as I said a little bit earlier, such screened material is absolutely essential for making the world's greatest potting soil for houseplants, window boxes, hanging baskets, and other containers! Just combine equal amounts of your screened compost, milled peat moss (the kind in those giant bricks; *NOT* whole, unshredded sphagnum moss, which resembles seaweed), and perlite (a natural mineral that's heated till it pops into little white balls that look like Styrofoam; this great lightweight potting and seed-starting ingredient is available in bags at all garden centers).

This mixture will create the *perfect* loose, light, but nutrient-rich growing medium for containers and houseplants. The plants in those containers will enjoy the looseness around their roots, you'll enjoy the light weight of the containers compared to if you had filled them with your heavy (and often potted-plant deadly) garden soil, and the compost in the mix will provide all the food the plants in those containers need for a full year!

Got some screened material left over after filling all your pots? Use it to make compost tea—which we'll discuss in just a few minutes. Or spread this highest-quality compost around your most important—and disease-prone—garden plants. (I hear people out there screaming "roses!!" You can add tomatoes and lilacs to that list as well.) But again, don't feel that you need to screen all your compost for everyday garden use; you don't—I certainly don't. Outside of being a necessity for container use, it's just a fun option.

OK—let's get to the actual feeding.

Now, if you live anywhere but the deep South, the best way to build up the nutrition and soil structure of your garden beds is to put a two-inch-thick layer of compost on top of the soil and then either till it in with a roto-tiller or turn it in with a big soil fork, mixing it well with the top six inches of what was already there. The best time to do this is late Fall; this will give soil microbes more time to unlock the nutrients in that compost and make them available to your plants the following season. It's also when you're likely to have the most finished compost available, because Summer is when compost gets made the fastest. *AND* it's when you should empty out all your old compost containers and get them ready for the Fall leaf largesse to come!

But you can mix your black gold into your soil anytime you and your compost are ready.

If that happens to be in the Spring, go right ahead and till it in in the morning; you can safely put *plants* in that bed the same evening. (You should *never* plant in the morning or afternoon; always put your plants in the ground late in the day, when they'll have time to get established before they have to endure their first day of bright sun. Plant them in the morning of what turns out to be a blindingly sunny day and they may lie down to take long naps—perhaps forever.)

If you're direct-seeding, either wait a week after mixing the compost in, or direct-seed, wait till the plants have been up and growing for two weeks, and then apply the compost as a mulch around them; some sensitive seeds don't like to be planted into fresh compost-enriched beds immediately.

And that's all the nutrition that bed should require for that entire season. In future years, a freshening up of an inch of new compost a season should be all your plants require—either mixed in again or just placed right on top of the soil. In the *North*, that is.

Down *South*, where the hotter temperatures and longer growing season conspire to use up your soil's organic matter at a much more rapid pace, you'll need more. The exact amount depends on how far South you are, but double is a good general rule for most of youse. That would be up to a four-inch layer mixed in at first and then a yearly "pick me up" of two inches. (We'll go into more detail about Southern helpings in a little bit.)

This type of application will achieve two of the three things that compost brings to the table...eh, garden:

1. It will greatly improve your soil structure, creating a richer, darker, more friable growing medium that both drains better *and* retains moisture more efficiently. And . . .

2. It will provide all the nutrition the plants in that bed need for a full year—*honest!*

Please don't go nuts and think, "Well—if *two* inches is great, *eight* inches will be four times better!" It won't be better. Plants don't enjoy being overfed any more than we people do, and there really *can* be "too much of a good thing," even with a natural fertilizer like compost.

Use a little bit of the compost you've made on *all* the plants in your landscape—and inside your home; don't forget those hungry houseplants!—before you even start thinking about giving your beds a second helping. Much better to set any extra compost aside and use it for compost tea if you want to give your plants a little mid-Summer boost, OK?

7 Using Compost to Prevent Plant Diseases

A big "note" here: Compost mixed into the soil does *not* have the disease-preventing and illness-fighting power that many find to be black gold's finest attribute.

Compost is *ALIVE*—so alive, that a single *teaspoon* can contain more than 100 million beneficial bacteria and other little critters. Some of these tiny helpers are responsible for improving the structure of the soil they're added to; others specialize in providing compost's nutrition to plants in a form they can utilize much more efficiently than the concentrated chemical salts in commercial fertilizers.

And many of compost's microscopic organisms—like the "Actinomycetes" (ack-tin-o-my-seats)—actively fight plant disease. Some are toxic to disease organisms; others compete for the same food as the disease; and some actually *EAT* the disease organisms directly (after all, those diseases *are* simply tiny living things themselves). Very, very cool.

But to defeat those diseases, the billions of little foo fighters in your compost must be exposed to those nasty organisms—and that's why there are special compost rules for disease-prone plants like the aforementioned tomatoes, roses, and lilacs. To best protect these plants—and any plants that regularly come down with the horticultural sniffles in your landscape—your compost should not be mixed into the soil. Instead, spread an inch of your best quality black gold right on the surface of the soil around your disease-prone plants at the beginning of the season, and then freshen up that layer with another quarter-inch every month or so. This will keep your living disease fighters in the perfect physical position to interrupt any developing illnesses before they can get a foothold.

…Because right down there on the ground is where diseases get started. Yes, we generally first *notice* disease on the plant itself. But by that time, it's been around for quite a while. Maybe the spores blew into your garden at some point, or maybe they were *already* lurking down on that soil, just waiting for *their* growing season to start. Those disease spores breed and flourish down there on the soil surface, and then get blown up onto the plant by wind or splash up onto it when it rains—in *large* numbers by then. Having fresh compost on the surface of that soil ensures those pesky spores will receive a very cold shoulder instead of a warm welcome.

For annual plants like tomatoes, spread the compost on the ground right after you put the young plants out. Spread enough compost to cover the area that will eventually be shadowed by the canopy of the plant when it is fully grown; for big heirloom and some cherry tomatoes, that's often a good three or four square feet! Freshen up that layer with a new quarter-inch of compost monthly during the growing season and/or give the plants regular sprays of compost tea—which we'll get to in just a bit.

For perennials like roses, it's crucial first to give the plants a good Spring pruning to remove any parts that show even the *slightest* signs of disease. (*NEVER* prune any plant in the Fall—especially in the North. It can weaken them, expose them to Winter injury, cause new growth that will kill the poor plant when it freezes solid, and lessen their cold hardiness in general.)

After that pruning, remove all the old mulch and debris from underneath the plant; that's where last year's disease spores are lurking. If there's no mulch down there *to* remove, scrape off the top quarter-inch of soil. Then apply that inch of fresh compost and freshen it up monthly during the season.

And what should you do with the diseased plant parts you just pruned off and all that old mulch you raked up? Throw it all in the trash, or toss it into wooded areas far, far away from your gardens. DO *NOT* compost this red-bag material; and don't re-use that mulch somewhere else in your landscape—no matter how safe it looks.

In fact, if you have enough black gold, and you're fighting a *REALLY* tough disease—like black spot on roses—consider removing and replacing even that *compost* mulch with a fresh inch every month during the growing season. I know it seems extreme, but you rose growers know how tough and troublesome some of these diseases can be—no chemical fungicide can stop them. But compost *CAN*—and the best way to fight the really *DREAD* plant diseases is with relentlessly fresh compost mulches.

Now do you see why we always say you can *never* make too much compost?

8 Compost for Trees and Shrubs

Most trees are pretty good at finding their own food—that's why they got them deep roots. But if you think your big guys really need a little nibble, just spread a half-inch of compost a year—no more than that—on the ground around the base of the tree, beginning at around six inches away from the trunk. If you want to give that tree a really good feeding, spread that half-inch as far out as the tree's furthest branches reach. And, as with all mulches, never actually touch the trunk of the tree. Whether it's compost or a traditional mulch—which trees do *NOT* need and are often harmed by; especially wood chip and shredded bark mulches—

STEP BACK
SIX INCHES AND
NO ONE GETS HURT!

nothing should *ever* touch the trunk; you want a good six inches of open area all the way around.

And yes, I **meant** what I just said about mulching trees; the best way is *NOT* to. If, for some reason, you feel you *MUST* mulch a tree—like a newly planted tree during a dry spell—use compost, shredded leaves or other non-wood material, keep the mulch at least six inches away from the trunk, and keep the layer of mulch itself two inches high or less. Any deeper than that and you'll start smothering the root system. Those "volcanoes" of piled mulch that have become so popular are tree *killers*!

Now, if you have a tree that's been attacked by disease in the past—for instance, a dogwood prone to anthracnose or other ills, follow our previous instructions for roses: Prune off any diseased parts in the Spring (feel free to wait till after flowering if it's a Spring blooming beauty), clean up and throw away all old mulch and debris you find underneath the tree, apply a half-inch of fresh compost to the surface of the soil, and freshen it up a couple of times during the growing season—more frequently in a wet and gloomy year, less often during a dry and sunny one.

With shrubs, I just like to toss a couple of shovelfuls of finished compost underneath the lowest branches every couple of seasons—*NOT* every year. Like trees, most shrubs don't *need* a lot to eat, and many actually prefer a poor soil. So do a little research first—if the plant in question *IS* a fairly *heavy* feeder, you can safely give it an inch of compost on top of the soil—that's generally a couple of shovelfuls—each year. But if that shrub is a *poor* soil champ, just a single shovelful, tops! Overfeed a plant that likes poor soil and it'll look awful for a while. Then it'll die.

Oh, and you don't have to worry too much about compost upsetting the *pH* of soils in which you're growing acid-loving plants like azaleas, rhododendrons, and blueberries. One of the really cool things about compost—and other forms of organic matter—is that they actually make the plants they're feeding less sensitive to *pH*.

That's right—an azalea, for instance, growing in soil that's never had the benefit of added compost *will* be very sensitive to that soil's *pH*; if that soil doesn't stay *highly* acidic, you'll probably lose that plant. But when the soil is rich in organic matter—especially in the form of compost—that very same azalea will thrive—even if the *pH* is approaching neutral! The more organic matter in the soil, the less the *pH* matters. And compost is organic matter on a stick, baby!

(If you have a *sickly* acid lover in your landscape, give it both: Put down an inch or two of milled peat moss to lower the *pH* naturally, and then cover that with an inch of compost to provide organic matter— and to keep the light-in-weight peat moss from blowing away. Azaleas, rhododendrons, and blueberries love receiving such thoughtful care— even when they aren't sick!)

9 Compost for Lawns

First, I want to expound on that little secret I revealed earlier in the book: The single most important thing you can do to have a healthy, great-looking lawn has nothing to do with chemicals *or* organics—it's the cutting height of your mower.

Almost all Americans cut their grass too short—often in the mistaken belief that they then won't have to cut as often. It's actually the reverse; the lower you cut your lawn, the more often you'll end up mowing it. Remember that grass blades are *PLANTS*, and *all* plants need to absorb solar energy to fuel the growing process. When you scalp your turf, you remove *WAY* too much of the green portion of the grass—the part that captures the sun. The grass responds in a panic—sending up weak green shoots much too rapidly in a desperate attempt to capture some sunshine. Of course, such growth looks ratty and uneven, which makes the lawn look like it needs mowing. So you scalp it again a week later, maybe even foolishly going lower.

Most American grasses should be two inches high (warm-season grasses for the South, like Bermuda and Centipede) to three or three and a half inches high (cool-season grasses in the North, like Kentucky blue and the fescues, respectively)— *—AFTER THEY'RE CUT*.

That's right—*after*. Buy a ruler, OK?

PERFECT!

-5"
-4"
-3"
-2"
-1"

Many wonderful things happen when you raise the cutting height on your mower to such levels. No longer in a panicky state, the lawn relaxes. New growth is now lush, full, and stocky—no more of those tall, leggy shoots of uneven grass that are a sure sign of sunshine deprivation.

The grass will also grow much more slowly now—at its *natural* rate, which is much slower than that of a scalped lawn. You might now only need to mow once a month instead of once a week. And best of all, the grass can now devote the energy it was wasting on shooting up those weak blades of desperation to doing what grass does best— growing deep, thick, tenacious roots that no weed has a chance against.

That's right—weeds. The single biggest cause of lawn weeds is grass that's cut too low.

When allowed to prosper, grass roots are unbeatable—they take over every inch of their underground growing space, leaving no room for new weeds and squeezing out existing ones. (The grass in a fescue lawn, for instance, that's cut to three inches high will have 18-inch-long roots. Sounds pretty good, eh? Let it grow just another half-inch to its recommended height and those roots will go down *four feet.*)

And that newly happy, thick, and lush *above-ground growth* provides its own double barrier—preventing weed seeds from reaching the soil, and shading out any new competition that *does* make it down there to sprout.

And the overall look of the turf will improve as well. Lawns that are cut at their correct height look much *better* than scalped ones.

Now, if you use a mulching mower—a machine that captures the cut blades, pulverizing them into a dust-like powder that's returned to the turf—you're already providing about half the food your lawn needs. Those grass clippings are powerful sources of nitrogen—the primary food for turf. If they were bagged and sold as fertilizer, those mulched clippings would rate an impressive 10-1-1 nutrient count on the label. That's right—they're 10 percent nitrogen! And that's about as good as a natural fertilizer gets.

Compost is the ideal food to provide the rest of your lawn's nutrient needs. And it's surprisingly easy to apply. I know—I did it. And I was surprised at how easy it was to do!

Fall is when lawns in the North should receive their biggest feeding of the year (cool-season grasses, that is; if you're growing a warm-season grass like zoysia in a cool climate, follow the warm-season feeding plan). And that Fall feeding *should* be with compost. After all, this time of year—the end of Summer—is when you should have the most black gold available, thanks to the warm weather helping your batches cook up quickly.

If you mulch your clippings back into your lawn, apply a half-inch of compost to the surface. If you do *NOT* return those mulched clippings to your turf, make it an inch. (I'll tell you how to translate things like pounds and cubic feet into "spread inches" later in the book.)

The application is *VERY* simple and easy to do—just put the compost into a wheelbarrow and dump out regular small amounts or shovelfuls as you roll up and down the lawn. Don't worry too much about precision here; just get it all on the lawn. Then rake those small piles onto the areas around them until it seems fairly even or all the compost disappears, which it often will.

Water it in gently; just a little bit. Then water some more an hour later—again, only for a few minutes. Repeat this several times and then back off and allow the liquid you've created—essentially compost tea—to feed the roots.

The compost itself will slowly break into smaller particles and work itself down under the lawn and into the soil, improving the structure of the earth under your grass. That's right—feeding your lawn with compost improves the soil structure underneath. Like I've been saying, this is pretty miraculous stuff.

You'll be very happy with how your turf responds. Instead of going into shock from being bombarded with heavily concentrated chemical salts, your lawn will simply have access to all the nutrients it needs—including minerals and trace elements completely missing in chemical lawn fertilizers—in a form the grass can absorb naturally, as needed, at its own pace. It really is the perfect lawn food. And you won't see any compost on the lawn the next day. (If you *DO*, it's because you missed a pile! Just go back and rake it around a bit.) It disappears completely.

Now, be aware that this is very *special* **watering** advice, *only* for after-compost use. If you're able, continue your short waterings— preferably in the early morning—for the next few days after applying compost. Water the grass for five or ten minutes, stop, repeat an hour later, stop, and repeat again. This will get the nutrients in the compost right to your roots for a quick feeding that the solid material can then follow up on more slowly. Don't allow any runoff during this time; you don't want to waste any of that precious compost! If it rains, back off your watering. (And don't apply this big feeding if downpours are predicted the next couple of days. Drizzles are fine—perfect, in fact; then you won't have to be doing your daily watering dance.)

But be sure and water *correctly* the rest of the year. That means deep and infrequently.

When you go a week without rain during the growing season, apply an inch of water to the lawn overnight. Typically that means turning your sprinklers on around midnight and off around 6 AM. (Yes—it takes a *LONG* time to achieve an inch. Test it yourself—put a rain gauge out there and run your sprinkler till it hits the inch line; in most cases, it'll take about six hours.)

*IN*frequent, *deep* waterings help your turf establish the deep, thick roots that crowd out weeds; this style of watering is the best way to keep a lawn happy. If you were to only water your lawn in short bursts (as it's *OK* to do after applying compost), you'd stunt the growth of your lawn's roots.

Spring is the other time to feed a Northern (cool-season grass) lawn; but it can be tough to do this with compost in many parts of the country. It simply gets too cold over the Winter to make compost quickly, *AND* you'll probably need all the compost you *DO* have for all those plants going into your Summer garden. Now, if you *do* have enough or don't mind buying a nice load of high-quality compost, go ahead and repeat that Fall feeding exactly; you'll be building the best possible soil under your sod.

But if you don't have enough compost or are battling weeds like crabgrass, use corn gluten meal for the Spring feeding instead. This all-natural material is a by-product of cornstarch manufacture. Its

YES! THE BREAKFAST of CHAMPIONS!

naturally high nitrogen content—10 percent, about the same as grass clippings themselves—makes it a perfect lawn food.

But corn gluten meal also has a unique attribute. As discovered by Dr. Nick Christians at Iowa State University in the late 1980s, corn gluten meal with a *very* high protein content also prevents weed seeds from sprouting—and that means no new crabgrass or any of the other troublesome weeds that germinate in Spring. Apply 10 to 20 pounds of corn gluten meal (identified on the label as a pre-emergent herbicide) per thousand square feet of lawn and you'll give that grass a good feeding and prevent weed seeds from sprouting. Apply it just as your forsythia starts to bloom—that's the perfect time to get those crabgrass seeds before they can sprout. (Crabgrass germinates after about five days of 55°F. soil temps in the Spring; if there is no forsythia in your area, ask your local county extension agent when crabgrass tends to germinate in your region. In the Washington, D. C., area, for instance, it's generally around the Ides of March.)

Now, *because* it prevents seeds from sprouting, you can't use corn gluten meal at the same time you seed a new lawn or reseed an old one. But that's fine—you Northerners with cool-season lawns should do all your grass seeding in the Fall anyway. Cool-season grass seed sown in Fall in the North has a much higher survival rate than Spring-sown seed. (Summer-sown grass just dies, period.)

You can find corn gluten meal in bags at many garden centers. Make SURE it's marked "organic weed and feed," "natural pre-emergent herbicide," or other such wording; some rural stores carry corn gluten meal that's designed to be used as animal feed, and the protein level of the lower-quality material will not prevent weed-seed germination. The real thing is also available mail order from "Gardens Alive!" the company that first marketed the product; they call their brand "WOW," for "With Out Weeds."

And if you'd like to read the fascinating research behind "organic weed and feed," go to this Iowa State University web site: (http://www.gluten.iastate.edu/)

Southern, warm-season lawns should *NOT* be fed in the Fall; their grasses are about to go dormant then, and you never want to feed a plant that's dormant or about to become so. Instead, Southern, warm-season turfs should receive three roughly equal feedings: in June, July, and August. Corn gluten meal is fine for any of these as long as you're not seeding or reseeding right then. (To grow or re-seed a warm-season grass down South, you should always spread your seed in the Spring.) Otherwise, compost is the ideal food for any—or all—three feedings.

Now, as we mentioned earlier, organic matter burns up faster in climes that warm up early and stay warm longer. I garden in Pennsylvania. By the time we get down to southern Virginia, organic matter is being used up twice as fast as it is at my place. By the time we get to Georgia, double again. And by the time we get to Phoenix, she'll be rising. (You saw that coming, didn't you?)

Seriously, down in Florida, they need four times the amount I use to compensate for the heat. But they also get to grow great plants year-round instead of taking four months off to clear ice dams from their roof.

Anyway, figure half- to three-quarters of an inch each feeding for the Upper South (almost a contradiction in terms to those of us who toil in the North, I realize—but you know who you are down there), an inch each time for the mid-South, and as much as an inch and a half down where "snow" is just a 7-point Scrabble word.

10 Compost as Mulch

I have been warning people for years that wood mulches—wood chips, shredded bark, sawdust, and those increasingly popular root mulches—can breed a nuisance mold that's known as "shotgun" or "artillery" fungus, that shoots tar-like spores as far as 30 feet toward light-colored objects, like the side of your house or car.

These spores can be removed pretty quickly if you get to them right away, explains Dr. Dan Herms from Ohio State University: Soak them thoroughly with soapy water for a few minutes to loosen the natural "glue" they exude, then scrub them off vigorously. But as I have always warned, once the spores *dry*, they are virtually impossible to remove without destroying the surface they're adhering to.

Wood mulches can also slow the growth of established plants—and yes, just plain starve new ones to death—by tying up the available

food in your soil, a process known as "Nitrogen immobilization." Wood is carbon; carbon always looks for nitrogen to bond with so it can break down into new soil—that's the principle behind composting. Wood mulches take that nitrogen right out of the soil, out-competing your nitrogen-needy plants.

And dyed mulches are the absolute *WORST* offenders. The wood in the old pallets that is used to make this mulch (they're chipped up and sprayed with dye) is the worst type for use around plants. Our favorite mulch expert, Ohio State Professor Emeritus Dr. Harry Hoitink, warns that dyed mulch is *especially* deadly when used around young plants or in brand-new landscapes.

Another problem occurs in the Spring, when sap-filled trees are chipped and shredded and the mulch sits around all piled up. Dr. Hoitink explains that this sap essentially becomes a high-strength vinegar, with a *pH* as low as 2.5; no plant can survive such an acidic attack. So *doubly* beware of wood mulch with a sour, vinegary smell.

Heard enough bad things about wood mulches yet? (If not, see the end of this chapter for links to Ohio State and Iowa State horticultural bulletins about these and others dangers caused by wood mulches.)

Seriously, wood mulches are one of the biggest problems in gardening today. Trees are always being cut down and/or trimmed, and the resulting wood waste costs big bucks to be landfilled, so municipalities and tree-trimming services prefer to give it away— always without any warnings about the potential dangers to your home and garden. (Chipped-up Christmas trees are even *WORSE*, as their "piney" sap can cause its own problems.) Wood chip and bark mulches *ARE* perfectly good for things like keeping weeds down in the pathways between raised garden beds, or smothering unwanted vegetation far away from homes and cars. But if you take only one thing away from this book, make it "wood mulch awareness." I get literally hundreds of e-mails every year from people whose gardens, homes, or cars were irrevocably harmed by wood.

So what *SHOULD* you use? Our *new* mulch maven Dr. Dan Herms (Harry is trying to retire and wants to pass his well-mulched torch along) warns *against* using one of my old favorites, straw. He says that straw is carbon-rich enough to cause some of the same plant-food-stealing problems as wood *and* that it often contains seed heads that can cause weed problems (which we've warned about in the past) *AND* that those seeds can attract rodents that will then look for other trouble to get into on your landscape (which I *hadn't* thought of before).

He does think highly of my *personal* mulch of choice, shredded Fall leaves—but doesn't think it's the absolute #1 choice. Both he and Harry feel confident that, after many years of active research, they have uncovered the *BEST* all-around mulch.

You ready? It's ***compost***.

Now, for years, I had been telling people that compost was a great soil improver, plant feeder, and disease fighter, but that it didn't qualify as "mulch" because it wouldn't prevent weeds. ***WRONG***, says Dr. Herms.

"In a recent study at Ohio State, we kept track of 'weeding hours' for plots that were mulched with either two inches of compost or ground wood, and there was no difference between the two," he reports. "Both mulches reduced weeding time to $1/20^{th}$ of that required to weed an un-mulched 'control' plot." So, solid university research now shows that two inches of compost controls weeds as well as a conventional wood mulch!

And Dr. Herms—who is *not* an organic researcher by any means (he used the nasty chemical herbicide Roundup to kill the existing weeds in his plots)—adds that their research clearly showed that compost mulch greatly enhanced plant growth, while wood mulches slowed it down or just plain killed the plants.

He also feels strongly that the look is just as attractive as dyed wood. "I now use compost to mulch everything in my home landscape," he told me. "The rich black compost really sets off the green of the plants and the colors of the flowers beautifully. In fact, it *looks* just like a dyed black mulch—but without any of wood's downsides."

Unlike wood mulches, you do have to apply to apply a fresh inch or two every year to keep weeds at bay. But Dr. Herms adds that the new compost will also greatly limit disease and insect problems in the plants it mulches *and* improve their overall vigor and root growth. Wood mulches, he notes, often have the opposite effect.

And, of course, it's the perfect double-duty mulch, since it does all those good mulch-ey things while feeding your plants.

And if you needed yet *more* assurance that compost really *CAN* provide all the food your landscape needs, Dr. Herms adds that their research uncovered something else that's verrrrryyyy interesting: "Adding fertilizer to plants mulched with compost had no effect at all; the plants simply didn't need any more food." Plants mulched with wood, of course, needed lots of added fertilizer.

So there's absolutely *no* excuse for risking your landscape, your home's siding, and your car's paint job with wood mulches. Many large garden centers have big piles of compost they'd be happy to deliver, just like wood and bark mulches. Give it the same "sniff, feel, look" test we told you to use on your own homemade compost (and check out the "buying compost" section later on in the book for more compost-to-consumer details).

Just remember to keep *ALL* mulches six inches away from the trunk or stalk of any plant; *any* mulch will rot a plant it's piled against. Keep all mulches six inches away from your home as well; subterranean termites will use *ANY* moisture-conserving cover—even stone—to reach your framing.

As promised, for more info on mulches, good and bad:
The very latest research, from Iowa State & Ohio State University:
http://www.extension.iastate.edu/Publications/SUL12.pdf
Dr. Harry Hoitink's classic bulletin on wood mulch problems from Ohio State; includes photos of shotgun fungus damage and other nuisance molds:
http://ohioline.osu.edu/hyg-fact/3000/3304.html
Dr. Hoitink's home page, with links to these and lots of other research articles on mulches:
http://plantpath.osu.edu/faculty/hoitink.php
Or just use your favorite search engine to search the terms "compost as mulch," "shotgun fungus," and "Dr. Harry Hoitink," and "Dr. Dan Herms" if you fear trying to transcribe those numbers, letters, and Klingon landing site symbols correctly; the right sites should be in the top couple of choices offered.

11 Time for Tea

Many of you out there like liquid fertilizers. Some of you are growing disease-prone plants in such dicey conditions that you need all the help you can get to keep horticultural illness at bay. And some of you, who think your plants need three meals a day and can't be deterred from this overfeeding idea, need a very gentle fertilizer that will help you feel like you're nurturing your plants enough while not turning them into the equivalent of 700-pound people.

Compost tea is the answer you're all looking for.

Take some of your absolutely finest finished compost—screened if possible—and place it in a porous cloth container. An old sock to brew up a gallon's worth. An old t-shirt, tied off at the openings, for a five-gallon bucket. An old pillowcase or smallish burlap bag to make up a barrel- or trashcan-size batch.

Fill up your container with cool water. (If you're using treated, city tap water, let it sit for 24 hours, stirring it vigorously a couple of times to help the chlorine escape.) Then place your compost-filled "tea bag" into the container and let it steep for 24 hours. When it's done, empty the contents of that tea bag into the garden or toss it back into your compost pile or tumbler. *Be prepared to use the tea immediately!* It's filled with living, disease-fighting organisms, and they will die off as they use up the oxygen in their water.

Your finished brewed tea should be the color of tea—or weak coffee. If it's as dark as the Italian-style roast I brew up (which is darker than dark chocolate), you can thin it out a bit, but you don't have to.

The easiest way to use your tea is to simply put some in a watering can and use it to water your plants—indoors or out. Substitute compost tea for regular water once a month during the growing season for your houseplants. Outdoors, pretty much the same—once a month will give your plants a nice growing-season boost.

If you're down South, where organic matter burns up quickly in the soil, you can do this more frequently—up to every two weeks in growing zones 8 and higher.

But many people prefer to use the tea to "foliar-feed" their plants. To do this, pour your tea through a strainer to remove any big pieces that would clog your sprayer. (If it still clogs, make a second pass through cheesecloth.) Then pour the tea into a dedicated sprayer—one that has never held chemicals of any kind—and spray the compost tea directly onto your plants' leaves first thing in the morning. Yes, the *morning*—that's when the pores of those plants are open and receptive to moisture. As the sun rises, the plants open up to drink the dew on their leaves. Don't waste your time spraying in the heat of the day—by then, those pores have closed up tight to help the plants retain moisture. Really soak those leaves on both sides; don't worry about runoff—the roots will take that right up.

If you have plants that are prone to disease, spray them first and more heavily, making **sure** you spray the undersides of their leaves. If you have a limited amount of tea, spend it all on your roses, lilacs, tomatoes, dogwoods, and other plants prone to illness. The living creatures in the tea will deter disease before it can get a foothold.

If you have plants that are *ALREADY* diseased, follow the previously detailed plan: Prune off all visibly diseased parts, clean up and destroy all the old mulch under the plants, and *THEN* spray *HEAVILY* with the tea. *THEN* mulch around the base of the plants with an inch of fresh compost. This is a much more effective treatment than the most potent chemical fungicide.

If that *doesn't* keep disease at bay:

1. Have your soil tested. It's possible that the *pH* and/or nutrient levels are so out of whack that they're weakening the plants beyond hope.

2. Improve airflow to the area. Open up the centers of the plants themselves and prune or remove nearby trees, plants, and shrubs that are preventing the passage of air.

3. Move the plants so they receive morning sun. Disease-prone plants need to have their leaves dry off as quickly as possible in the morning. If they sit in shade till noon, nothing will save them.

4. Take up woodworking.

Remember to use all your compost tea quickly; "within 24 hours" is the basic rule, but sooner is always better. And, you know, the more I think about it, the more that "24 hour rule" sounds suspiciously like "Aquaman" talk. Remember that old DC Comics superhero—the King of the Sea and his Finny Friends? All DC super-folk needed to have a special weakness to help the writers, so Supes ("The Big Blue Boy Scout)" had Kryptonite; Green Lantern's ring couldn't affect anything yellow; the Martian Manhunter couldn't stand fire, and "if Aquaman remains out of water for 24 hours he perishes!" So, of course, three-quarters of the Aquaman stories during my childhood had him stranded in the middle of a desert at 23 hours and 50 minutes out of the water, looking just fine so far, but apparently fated to drop over and turn into dust in ten minutes and one second.

Even as a ten-year-old it was obvious to me that good old "A-Man" would probably suffer *progressively* from his aqua-detachment and be in pretty sad shape by say, hour twelve. In a desert with ten minutes left to go, he probably wouldn't be able to *MOVE*, much less take the tiny little individual canisters of compressed hydrogen and oxygen gas out of his hollow belt buckle (*EVERY* DC hero had a hollow belt buckle—except Batman who had the coolest belt in the world and didn't need one, and Wonder Woman, who terrified me), turn them on, hold a match in between, and make water.

The same is going to be true for all the little guys in your Justice League of Compost Tea. Most will probably be dead long before 24 hours is up.

So I suggest you start brewing at 7 AM on a Saturday morning. Remove the bag 24 hours later and start spraying immediately. You'll be applying the most-lively tea possible at the perfect time of day. Sure, you can make it at night, remove the bag the next night and then spray early the next morning—but by then, a lot of the living organisms that provide the disease-fighting power of compost tea will have passed away from lack of oxygen. (Unless they steal Aquaman's belt.)

Much better to begin the brewing early on "Morning one" and then spray early on "Morning two." Do that, and you'll see disease organisms packing little bitty bags and scurrying out of the garden on "Morning three."

And that's just *BASIC* compost tea. There are two tricks I'll teach you in the next section—fermentation and super-aeration— that can greatly *INCREASE* the disease-fighting power of this fabulous brew.

But be assured that you've now heard all the basics and are hereby entitled to be recognized as an esteemed graduate of the *You Bet Your Garden* College of Composting Knowledge. Know ye by all these presents that you are an ER (Educated Rotter)!

In which we examine premium compost teas and biological activators, seaweed, wood scraps, and other unusual ingredients; figure out how much compost equals an inch-deep layer—and answer the most common composting questions.

12 Advanced Compost Teas

As you recall, in our last thrilling episode, we explained how to put some compost into a porous cloth container and soak it in water for 24 hours to create compost tea—a classic liquid fertilizer that gardeners have relied on for decades to feed their plants and fight disease in their gardens.

Such regular ol' compost tea is great stuff. Whenever my plants need a little boost—especially my home-schooled . . . eh, I mean home-STARTED tomato and pepper seedlings when they reach drinking age (four weeks or so after appearing)—I make them a nice cuppa tea. It's easy, it's fast, and they get a very nice meal. But over the past few years, the science of compost tea has grown by leaps and bounds, and some genuine improvements have taken place—specifically "aerated" compost tea and fermented compost tea. Let's discuss the *fermented* type first.

In 1989, German researchers found that compost tea that was allowed to ferment seemed much more effective at fighting plant disease than regular compost tea. A 1994 Israeli study confirmed this earlier research. The Israeli crop scientists found that the fermented tea controlled downy and powdery mildews, some really tough molds, and even late blight; in some cases providing up to an astounding 90 percent drop in disease severity.

Since then, other studies—and the experiments of many organic gardeners—have yielded the same results. When you're facing really tough disease problems, fermented compost tea may be the single most effective remedy of any kind.

Here's a recipe for fermenting your own compost tea, based on how the Israeli researchers did it: Fill a bucket with five parts water to one part compost, cover with mosquito-proof screening, and place outdoors in a shady spot for 10 to 14 days. Scum will form on the

surface. Skim off as much of this scum as possible when you're ready to use the tea and pour the bulk of the remainder through a strainer into another bucket, stopping when solid stuff from the bottom begins to pour thru (you'll have a good amount of solid stuff in the bottom). Allow this liquid to settle out for an hour or so, so the sediment can drop down to the bottom of the bucket. Then use a scoop or measuring cup to fill your sprayer with the liquid that's risen to the *top*, avoiding the sediment on the bottom that would clog your sprayer.

If you're attempting to prevent a recurring disease before it starts, simply soak the plants well with morning sprays of the fermented tea, making sure to coat the undersides of the leaves and the center of the plants. If disease is already obvious, remove as much of the diseased parts as you can, and then spray. You can do this as often as every two to three weeks.

Fermented compost tea ("FCT" for short) is a powerful cure for black spot on roses. I once had a plant that was so vulnerable to this dread disease that it always died back to the ground before the end of Summer. Then one year, I got fed up. I pulled the whole plant out of the ground in early Spring, dunked it into a bucket of fermented compost tea and scrubbed the woody growth hard with the FCT, using an old toothbrush to really grind away at the outside of the plant. Then I cleared away the old mulch, replanted the rose, laid down the requisite inch of fresh compost, sprayed FCT on it every two weeks, and it didn't show a single spot of darkness on its leaves until August. I know of no chemical fungicide that could do half as good a job.

Oh, by the way, as with regular compost tea, you should toss all your leftovers—the scum, strained-out material, and the sediment from the bottom of the buckets—back into your composting pile or drum; there's still plenty of good stuff in there!

Now, a newer item on the scene is "aerated" or "oxygenated" compost tea. A number of names are used to describe this "supercharging," but the idea is very basic: Simply inject air into the process as you brew up a batch of compost tea—maybe with additional food to support the increased microbial growth the extra oxygen will stimulate.

As we've been saying all along, compost is alive. Your finished black gold is teeming with billions of tiny life forms, many of which attack disease organisms in a number of different ways—and all of which add critical life to your soil. That's why it's so important to use freshly brewed regular old compost tea *quickly*—those living organisms are using up the oxygen in the liquid, and the sooner you use it, the more life you'll apply to your plants and plots.

As people began to better understand the importance of using their tea while the oxygen levels were still high, the question arose—what about *adding* oxygen to the water? This was likely first done—using simple home aquarium bubblers—just to see if the tea could maintain its life levels longer. But it was soon discovered that more oxygen equaled *MORE* life, not just stability for the life that was there.

It turns out that the relative lack of oxygen in those buckets of water was *greatly* limiting the number of lively organisms that could colonize the tea. Forcing air into the brewing tea raised the oxygen levels enough to let the *maximum* number of beneficial little thingies develop—which turns out to be **many** times more than a normal tea's oxygen levels can support.

The science behind this is pretty astounding: Researchers have found that keeping the little guys well-aerated can lead to amazing increases in their numbers—10,000 to 50,000 *times* as many beneficial organisms as in the same size batch of non-aerated tea.

Several years ago, entrepreneur Ed Neff of Seattle helped design a sophisticated system that aerated *and* stirred the steeping compost tea to create what he calls "Soil Soup." Concerned that all those additional creatures would need extra *food* as well as air, the Soil Soup process included the use of a specialized nutrient solution—a blend of high-nitrogen seabird and bat guanos with some other nutrients in a base of molasses—to feed and fortify all the microscopic garden helpers rapidly multiplying in the beneficial brew.

If you'd like to try and utilize this advanced tea-brewing knowledge on your own, make up a batch of compost tea just like I learned ya how to a little ways back, but with anywhere from one to four of those little home fish tank aquarium bubblers pumping air into the bottom of the bucket via those porous stones. And because you are now breeding many, many more living things by shooting all that extra oxygen in there, you may also want to supply some extra food for your little friends as well. It's your choice; "without food" is perfectly acceptable as well.

If you're doing this yourself, as opposed to using one of the commercial systems out there, I'd suggest loosely following the directions and formulas the Soil Soup people recommend. Put about two cups of your finest finished compost into a porous cloth container (like a big old sock). Put that into a five-gallon bucket filled with cool, clean water, turn on your bubblers, and if you choose to feed, add half a cup of molasses (and if you have it, a couple of tablespoons of bat or seabird guano) directly to the water. Brew your tea for 24 to 36 hours, stirring as frequently as possible, and then use *immediately,* as you would any compost tea.

Of course, you can also buy devices that do the aerating and, in some cases, stirring for you. The Soil Soup folks, for instance, are one of several companies that sell brewing systems ranging in size from homeowner buckets to giant ones used by nurseries and garden centers; and they offer their nutrient solution for sale as well.

Now, they *also* say to *only* use worm bin compost to make your tea, but that's not why we're here, is it duckies? No—you can use their mixers and nutrient solutions, but that's going to be *YOUR* finest finished compost in that sock or customized cloth holder!

13 Compost Calculations

I'm always telling people in the North to (and I *quote*): "spread an inch of compost a year" on their lawn, garden, and other parts of their landscape to provide the perfect amount of natural nutrition. And, as we said earlier, that rises to more inches of compost as you head progressively South, where the heat and longer growing season use those nutrients up more quickly.

But how much *IS* an inch!? You can't spread all your compost out nice and even on a flat surface like a patio, get it to just the right height and then telepathically move it all over to your lawn! (Well, *I* can't, anyway—and believe me, I've tried!) So you need to be able to figure out the equivalents of that inch worth.

Here are a number of ways to calculate that precious inch.

If you have a scale, use it to weigh your black gold. On average, 40 pounds of compost equals about one cubic foot in volume. One cubic foot will cover twelve square feet an inch deep. So your most basic measurement is: 40 pounds = 1 cubic foot = 12 square feet of 1-inch coverage.

TAKE TWO INCHES of COMPOST and CALL ME in the MORNING.

You can also dump the compost into a wheelbarrow whose cubic volume you know and work from there. Most standard wheelbarrows hold about six cubic feet, which would cover seventy two square feet an inch deep.

Or pile up your compost and measure it. The height times the width times the depth equals the cubic volume. You need a little over eight cubic feet (8.3 to be exact)—that's a wheelbarrow and a third—to cover 100 square feet of lawn or garden an inch deep.

Or fill up standard five-gallon buckets with your finished material; a bucketful will contain about two-thirds of a cubic foot, which will cover eight square feet an inch deep.

Got some *real* bushel baskets? A standard American bushel contains one and a quarter cubic feet of material, which would cover about fifteen square feet an inch deep.

And finally, if you fill a standard 4 x 4 x 4-foot wooden slatted bin (the Lehigh style) all the way to its four-foot-high top with raw materials and then allow that material to compost down, it should reduce in size by half and now contain a two-foot-high batch of compost in a four-by-four square; 4 x 4 x 2 =32 cubic feet of compost, which should cover about 384 square feet an inch deep.

Whoa! Nobody warned me there'd be math today!

Seriously, don't go getting all nuts with slide rules and calculators here. I would worry about you if you were out there measuring your black gold like it was gold *dust*. Just have a good ballpark idea of how much you'll need for a specific application. And once you begin to actually spread the stuff, don't worry—just do your best and things will average out over time. It's compost—not rocket science! (Especially when I'm in the room.)

14 What About Seaweed?

Good question! Glad I asked it! Seriously, we've all heard stories about the benefits of using seaweed in the garden, and we've all seen numerous organic fertilizer products out there containing seaweed and kelp as ingredients. So what *about* incorporating seaweed into our compost? And is kelp something different?

The answer to the first question is yes; you absolutely *should* incorporate some seaweed into your compost if you can—and if it's the *right* kind. Seaweed contains trace elements, micro-nutrients, and plant growth compounds you'll never find in any chemical fertilizer— or even in most organic ones. Research performed at Clemson University found that seaweed contained at least 70 trace elements vital to plant growth—in just the tiny amounts plants like best.

The plant-growth compounds in seaweed can speed up flowering and fruit production and help plants better resist stress—especially the stress of cold weather. Some studies have found that regular applications of seaweed-based sprays can help plants survive temperatures a couple of degrees lower than they could normally when frost comes a-calling.

Seaweed can really boost yields as well—one study found that seaweed-fed plants produced a third more tomatoes than non-seaweeded plants (has my poor copy editor had a stroke yet?); and in another study, seaweed increased strawberry yields an astounding 133 percent! Yow!

Seaweed also helps plants better resist disease, and even lengthens the amount of time picked crops can be stored without loss of quality.

But, as I mentioned a bit earlier, it has to be the right *kind.* Seaweed from warm waters doesn't supply much—if any—of these benefits. In fact, some scientists call the plant life from really warm waters "trash seaweed" in terms of its agricultural potential. You want seaweed from **cold** waters; the colder the better. All the seaweed harvested to make commercial organic fertilizers comes from ocean waters so chilly you wouldn't last five minutes if you fell in.

So if you swim in the warm waters of say, Texas or Virginia, leave the seaweed at the beach. But if your ocean crashes against the rocky shores of say, New England, haul home any you can find—it's premium plant food.

And what about kelp? Technically, "kelp" is a specific term that identifies a large family of brown seaweed varieties. It's also used to define a large mass of any kind of seaweed. But in reality, seaweed and kelp are terms used pretty much interchangeably in the world of plant food labels.

If you are lucky enough to live near really cold ocean waters— bbbrrr! wait a minute, let me rethink that one...sorry. Anyway, if you *do* have access to seaweed from cold waters, collect it, bring it home, pile it up, rinse it a little bit to remove any surface sea salt (it's actually much less salty than you might imagine), then use it as green matter in your compost. The compost you create from a mix that incorporates cold-water seaweed will be some of the most beneficial you can apply to your plants. If possible, use it to make compost tea, and use that tea on plants that are under stress or about to be stressed. Or just ones you want more ~~lots~~ tomatoes and strawberries from.

Oh, and plants that grow in *non*-ocean waters are great compost ingredients as well. "Cat tails" and other pond plants are rich in minerals and micro-nutrients that land-lubbing plants crave. The esteemed J. I. Rodale, who brought the science of composting to America, especially prized aquatic plants in his personal compost piles.

SEAHUNT

15 Wood Shavings and Sawdust?

O ne of the most frequent questions I hear is, "Can I use sawdust and/or wood shavings as the 'brown material' in my compost?" Woodworkers and carpenters generate a lot of sawdust and shavings, and they and their gardening friends often figure: "Hey, wood used to be *trees,* right? So this stuff *HAS* to be great to mix into your garden and compost piles, right?"

Actually, ***wrong***. (Or, as my old friend Elmer Fudd would say, "*werry, werry* wong.")

If you mix sawdust into your garden soil, nothing will grow there for a year or more. That's because pure wood materials are *super*-high in carbon, and their carbon will absorb all the plant-feeding nitrogen in your soil in its quest to decompose. After it *DOES* decompose, the soil *WILL* be richer, but for that first year it'll be a plant graveyard.

And compost making? As we've been saying all along, the best compost is made by combining carbon-rich dry brown material, like shredded Fall leaves, with wet green nitrogen-rich stuff, like grass clippings, kitchen waste, and manures. Now, wood shavings and sawdust *are* "dry brown" material, but they are *much* more highly concentrated forms of carbon than leaves.

When you combine the recommended four parts of shredded leaves and one part green waste, it's fairly easy for pretty much all of the dry brown material to come into contact with pretty much all of the green waste so the composting process can move along quickly. But when you're talking *sawdust*, you have to limit yourself to *VERY* small amounts of this ultra-high-carbon material to avoid going way out of whack on approximating a correct 30-to-1 carbon-to-nitrogen ratio.

I'd guess that if you were using regular kitchen waste for your green material, the correct ratio would be a cup or two of sawdust to

about ten gallons of garbage (two five-gallon buckets full). It just wouldn't work—there isn't enough volume of carbonaceous material to touch most of the garbage and start the composting reaction going.

Yes, *theoretically*, you could mix up something like a gallon of sawdust or wood shavings with a five-gallon bucket of *very* hot green material like seafood shells or blood meal, move it around constantly and get it to cook into (a pitifully small amount of) compost, but I wouldn't try it personally; the risk of (VERY stinky) failure is extremely high.

And using wood stuff is even *MORE* impractical with kitchen waste and other fairly low nitrogen materials. I can't imagine trying it in an open pile. You could *try* incorporating sawdust or wood shavings into a green-waste-filled drum system and mix the contents several times a day—but you probably still wouldn't like what you got. (I've heard from *many* gardeners who've tried it, and they warn that the garbage just sits there—the process is stopped *cold*.)

BUT—this does *NOT* mean that you can't compost your wood waste! You *can*—just not the way you've been thinking. Wood *IS* a natural substance and *will* become a soil-like material—but not in the average home compost pile or drum system. Instead, give your wood waste its own bin—with open sides, if possible—and allow it to break down naturally, which could take years. (As with all piles, the stuff on the bottom will be ready first).

You can greatly reduce the time involved by mixing in some nitrogen-rich material and turning the contents of the bin on a regular basis. As we mentioned earlier, Starbucks stores have that "Grounds for Gardeners" program where they give away their used coffee grounds in five-pound sacks. Those free grounds are very nitrogen rich (and they're free—did I mention that?).

Other high-nitro items you could use include blood meal (available bagged at garden centers), crab and shrimp shells, and bat and seabird guanos (also available bagged, but only at the coolest garden centers—you generally have to buy them mail order. Or shovel out the Bat Cave while Bruce Wayne's bat-butler Alfred is on vacation).

Poultry manures are also very hot, but you never get *just* the manure; it always comes mixed with the animal's bedding—shredded newspaper, straw, or, yes—wood shavings! (As we mentioned earlier, the word "manure" actually means a mixture of bedding materials *and* all that stuff the animal was done with.) Those high-carbon beddings already provide all the carbon the nitrogen-rich animal waste needs to compost nicely. So don't mix these already-woody-enough manures in with your woodworking leftovers; just pile them up all by their lonesome and enjoy the premium compost they make. Add them to a pile of shavings or sawdust and you'll have way too much carbon.

(NOTE: This is why it's really "shorthand" when we say that animal manures are one of the two things you can compost alone, because what *WE* think of as manure is almost never available alone—it always comes with bedding, making the "by itself" part of the statement more semantics than absolute truth.)

So experiment and be patient—and remember that your wood waste is *HUGELY* carbonaceous. No matter *what* you do, it will take a while to break down, and *only **very** rich sources of nitrogen will help it do so faster. This is *no* place for your kitchen scraps.

I suggest you just pile up that wood waste in a long-term bin, mix in any free high-nitrogen materials when you can find them, and be patient. Yes, it *is* wood, and yes, all wood *will* eventually rot and release its wonderful nutrients for your use. As with all compost, it's ready to use when it looks like nice, rich, black super-soil.

Oh, and I would hope that this is obvious, but *don't* use any shavings, sawdust, or scraps from pressure treated wood (which is brimming with arsenic and plant-killing levels of copper and chromium), old railroad ties (which are treated with creosote—one of the few substances science has found that unequivocally causes cancer—and/or a potentially nastier chemical, pentachlorophenol, often just referred to as "penta"), or other toxic wood in your pile. And don't use those toxically treated woods to make a bin. You're probably already meeting your RDA of arsenic. (For more info on the dangers of treated wood, visit the fabulous website "Beyond Pesticides" and choose "Wood Preservatives" from the "Issues" menu.

Oh, and a word about wood *ASHES* too. Lots of folks burn wood for heat and for fun, and often add the ashes to their compost piles—

without asking me *first;* they always call the show, tell me what they've done, and ask to be reassured that it was a good thing.

Well, it wasn't.

Wood ashes are *highly* alkaline; too much of 'em can raise *pH* to levels that stop composting cold—or kill garden plants, when they're applied directly. Small amounts are fine—the ashes of high-quality hardwoods (the only kind of wood you should burn for indoor heat) *DO* contain high levels of calcium and potassium, which are essential plant nutrients. But we are talking *small* amounts! No more than a cup of ashes mixed into a 4 x 4 x 4-foot bin. And that's just to placate you wood stove owners. Half a cup is closer to the limit that I—also a wood stove owner—place on my own piles.

It's much better to save up those ashes and use them instead of lime if a soil test reveals your lawn or garden soil could use a bump up the *pH* scale. If your soil does test acidic (which is common in areas with heavy rainfall), the test report will likely suggest you add a certain amount of lime to a certain square footage of garden or turf to raise the *pH* to the generally desired 6.5 level that the majority of plants prefer. You can instead apply one and a half times as much hard wood ash (by weight) as lime was called for to raise the *pH* to that number. If you use a home test kit or for some other reason don't get a "liming recommendation" with your results, contact your local extension agent for advice.

pH You're going to hear the term "*pH*" used every once in a while in this book. The *pH* of a substance is a measure of its acidity or alkalinity. Low numbers—under a *pH* of 7—are acidic. Numbers higher than 7 are alkaline. (7 itself is neutral.)

All soil tests check for *pH*; it is the most basic thing you should know about your soil. You can also buy strips that test for *pH* alone (similar to the ones used to check swimming pool water) and meters with probes that will reveal the *pH* of your soil.

Most plants prefer a slightly acidic soil—6.5 is the number that's thrown around quite a bit. Some of our most popular plants—azaleas, rhododendrons, blueberries, etc.—require a *very* acidic soil, a *pH* of 5 or 5.5. A few plants like it alkaline, but they're the exception.

Generally, if you live in the North, your soils tend naturally toward the acidic. High levels of rainfall (and the infamous acid *IN* some of that rain) tend to push *pH* levels down. That's why lawn owners frequently "lime" their turf in the North—using the alkaline lime to bring the *pH* closer to the neutral area that most grasses prefer. If you have a wood stove, use the ashes for this instead—they're better than lime, just as alkaline, and free.

Out West, where alkaline deposits are more common and rainfall more scarce, the soils tend to be alkaline. The most natural cure for such soils is to apply lots of peat moss to bring that number down. Obviously, wood stove owners in such areas *don't* want to use their ashes in compost-making or garden-soil-amending, because they would make their alkaline soil even more alkaline—unless they want to try selling a new version of "Death Valley Days" to TV, of course. They CAN use those ashes horticulturally, however—as a "killing mulch" for unwanted plants like thistle and kudzu!

16 Alternatives to Leaves as Dry Brown Material

This is always an issue—even for an experienced composter like me. Leaves are pretty much essential in a home composting system. They not only contain the right amount of carbon in the right size raw material to mix perfectly with your nitrogen-rich green waste, they also contain lots of trace nutrients and minerals the tree's roots have pulled up from deep in the earth.

That's why it's so important to collect, shred, and save as many Fall leaves as possible every season. You need to set aside enough of a supply to mix in with your green waste for an entire *year*. Remember—those leaves can be composted all on their own; *they* don't need anything else. But your wet greens—kitchen waste, spent garden plants, seed-free weeds, and clippings from an herbicide-free lawn—*NEED* leaves (or other dry brown matter) to compost down. Pile up shredded leaves alone and you'll get some really nice compost. Pile up kitchen waste alone and you'll get a pile of kitchen waste.

I know people who live in areas with very few deciduous trees—like Arizona—who locate clusters of the helpful plants and trek out to them every year when their leaves finally fall so they can collect the precious treasures for their composting operation, often keeping the location a closely guarded secret, like a prized patch of wild morel mushrooms.

Like them, you should do anything you can to ensure a supply of the real deal. If you live in an area where deciduous trees simply *don't*, maybe you can plan to visit friends or relatives in the Fall and return home with bags of shredded treasure. Or make them bring some bags to *you* when they come visit to escape their harsh Winter weather.

And don't *EVER* let a simple lack of trees on your *property* hold you back. Offer to rake up your friends' and neighbors' leaves if you can haul them away afterward. Find out how Fall leaf collection works in your area, and ask the township if you can have some after they collect a big batch. Heck—go leaf rustling! I live *IN* the woods and still never have enough leaves, so I keep the trunk of my car empty in the Fall and snatch any big bags of leaves I see set out for curbside pickup.

It's generally easy to figure out which bags contain treasure as opposed to trash. In most places, people have to buy and use special bags to put garden waste like leaves out for curbside collection. If you rustle such leaves, consider taking the bags home, emptying them out, folding them neatly, and giving that homeowner the bags *BACK* for reuse, saving them money. Heck, they may be willing to *call* you to come and get all their leaves after you explain they'll never have to pay for bags again! And some people bag their leaves up in clear plastic—making ID a cinch.

In one of the small cities close to where I live, the residents simply sweep their leaves into big piles, and a township truck comes along with a big vacuum device to suck them up. Not if I get there first! When I see those piles, I run to the store, buy a box of heavy-duty trash bags, and fill them up right from the piles. Sometimes—more and more often, in fact—I'll be lucky enough to find piles of *shredded* leaves; and that, of course is the bonus round. I can fit ten times as many in one bag when they're shredded—and I don't have to shred them myself later. Life is good.

So do everything you can to beg, borrow, steal, and stockpile lots and lots of leaves. You'll never get to the end of a Summer feeling you saved too many. (And if you actually *DO* manage to save too many, shredded leaves make a fabulous garden mulch!)

OK—now, one of the best alternatives to leaves is **straw**. I said "straw," *NOT* **hay**! Although both come in big bales and often look the same at first glance, there is a world of difference.

Straw is a giant compressed package of hollow plant stems (like its namesake the drinking straw) from which the seed heads have been removed. Bales of straw are used mostly for animal bedding. You layer the floor of an animal's stall with straw, the animals do what comes naturally, the straw collects that material, and then it's all swept out together; the straw keeping the floor much cleaner and much less slippery. (As we've said—how many times now?!—this mixture of straw and manure is perfect to compost all on its own—and the resulting compost will be very high quality.)

Hay, on the other hand, is meant to be used as fodder—animal feed. All of its seed heads are still intact, and it makes a weedy mess when used as garden mulch—a common rookie mistake. Those same seed heads are also a danger in your compost pile; you'd have to be *SURE* your compost heated up to 140 to 160 degrees—weed-seed cooking territory—before you could use the resulting compost without fear of it breeding a wheat field.

Don't trust signs, labels, or even the people selling the stuff—lots of folks simply use the terms interchangeably. Examine the bales carefully yourself. If you see many seed heads, pass those bales by. If you see few-to-no amber waves of grain, you've found true straw.

To use straw as brown matter in your composting system, break open the bales into their individual flakes—those square panels of compressed straw that make up a bale—and shred the flakes as much as you can. As with leaves, you can suck this material through the internal shredder in a blower/vac, run it over with your lawnmower, or run it through a shredder. Then use the shredded straw just as you

would leaves, in pretty much the same proportions; about four parts straw to each part kitchen waste or other wet green material.

Straw won't provide as many minerals and trace nutrients as leaves, but it will contain *some*. And perhaps more important if you live in the land of non-deciduousness, it will cook up a batch of compost just as quickly as leaves would.

Another option is the *BROWNED* remains of the previous year's passed-away garden plants. I used to say that folks who wanted to start composting in the *Spring*, but who hadn't saved lots of leaves to mix in with their wet greens like kitchen waste, were sunk till the Fall. But renowned compost expert Dr. Frank Gouin ("Go-in"), retired head of the Horticulture Department at the University of Maryland, recently taught me otherwise.

He explained that the browned-out tops of the previous year's perennials—like black-eyed Susan, Echinacea, ornamental grasses, and the like—are perfect Fall leaf substitutes. All their nitrogen has retreated to the *roots*, he explained—making those brown dead tops slightly *better*, in his opinion, than leaves for mixing with green waste! Gasp—I loined something new!

Now let's make sure you got this right—*NOT* such plants while they're still green (nitrogen-rich), but when they've been dead for a while and have turned brown—indicating that they've lost most of that nitrogen. (Nitrogen is a nutrient that's notoriously easy to "lose"—very unstable, it escapes back into the air very easily, which is why most soil tests don't even check for nitrogen content; it's really "here today; gone tomorrow" compared to more stable plant nutrients like potassium and phosphorus.)

The bigger and browner the better—think old cornstalks and the browned-out leaves and stems of last year's hostas, ornamental grasses, and the like. And, yes, those perennial tops *should* be there still standing in the Spring—especially the further north you are.

The top growth of perennials should always be left standing over Winter and removed the following Spring—for increased frost protection of the crown. (And to provide what Martha used to call "Winter interest" before she had to go up the river and make little doilies out of big doilies.)

The more dried-out and crunchy, the more usable your plant matter will be as a "dry brown" component of your pile. Just remember to shred whatever it is first—*EVERYTHING* that goes into your compost pile should be in the smallest pieces possible.

And what about ***paper***?

We're talking **no** added nutrition *whatsoever*, AND the possibility of adding lots of chemicals to your compost. Paper towels and napkins and such are often bleached with chlorine and contain dangerous dioxins. Shredded newspaper is not only bleached, there's also the issue of the inks used in printing. It's OK to include coffee filters (especially if you buy the unbleached brown paper versions) and the odd paper towel in the kitchen garbage component of your compost ingredients, but I wouldn't use compost that was made with *lots* of paper products. That compost would be hugely inferior in the nutrition it could offer your plants, would not have any disease-fighting power, and it would likely be contaminated with some fairly dangerous chemicals and their by-products.

If you *really* can't find any leaves, straw, or browned-out perennial parts, I'd suggest experimenting with wood shavings instead of turning to paper products. Yes, I **did** just say they're really problematic—but they haven't been bleached, and that's a big plus.

17 What About Leaves from the Dreaded Black Walnut!?

Ah, yes, the famous "killer tree."

Another frequent question I hear is if it's safe to use the leaves of this competition-crushing plant in compost-making. Darn good question.

The basics: Black walnut trees contain a natural substance called juglone that inhibits the growth of many nearby plants (or just plain kills them). It's contained in every part of the tree—bark, wood, leaves—but it is strongest in the *roots*. In fact, those roots are *SO* full of it that Dr. Paul Roth, Professor Emeritus in the Department of Forestry, Southern Illinois University, once warned me that a black

walnut's toxic effects on other plants will continue for several years if the roots are left in the ground. (And the trees are also good sprouters, which means that they will attempt to regrow after cutting, as well. So if you *do* decide to cut a walnut down, plan to have the stump pulled— *and* the ground-up chips taken away; those chipped-up roots would likely be the undisputed heavyweight champion of plant-killing wood mulches!)

The area over which walnuts affect sensitive plants generally extends at least 50 to 80 feet from the trunk, or about twice as far as the crown of the tree when it's fully leafed out. Plants noted for dying *quickly* within this range include the most popular home-grown veggies (tomatoes, peppers, eggplant, and potatoes) and ornamental favorites like petunias, azaleas, viburnums, hydrangeas, and rhododendrons. Blueberries too.

However, grasses—especially Kentucky bluegrass—are felt to *THRIVE* near the trees (as long as they get enough sun and water, of course). And a surprising number of other plants can also apparently coexist with black walnuts. The Ohio State University Extension office has compiled a two-page list of plants that don't *seem* to be affected (most of this information is based on observation, not hard research), including squash, melons, beans, carrots, and corn; clematis, forsythia, marigolds, begonias, violets, zinnias, and pansies (yay! I love pansies!); most Spring bulbs (double yay!), some daylilies, peonies, and hostas; and some fruit trees and arborvitae. (For the complete list go to: http://ohioline.osu.edu/hyg-fact/1000/1148.html. You'll also find lots of similar lists on the web.)

So, what *about* making compost with the leaves? The basic answer has always been not to worry about it if they're just a small component of your Fall leaf largesse (say, two or three trees out of a hundred on your property, or one tree out of ten or twenty).

Writing this book made me realize that I've been incorporating the leaves from a couple of black walnuts into my piles for the past two decades, and "so far, so good" (which, admittedly, is also what the guy who jumped off the Empire State Building is reported to have said as he passed the 40th floor...).

If you *can* largely isolate your black walnut leaves, however (they're very distinctively shaped), you may want to keep them out of the compost pile for deliberate use as a kind of horticultural Death Ray. Dr. Roth told me that he *does* personally make leaf-rich compost, but never puts *any* of his black walnut leaves in his piles; instead he saves them to use as a "killing mulch" to get rid of unwanted plants! *VERY* clever! (And as we said a minute ago, the chipped-up **roots** would be even *more* effective.)

Based on years of research, experts at Ohio State say that well-shredded walnut leaves generally lose their plant-harming capability after a month of hot composting. But if you have a *LOT* of black walnut leaves going into your pile and/or have a tomato-heavy garden, they suggest you test the finished compost by planting some extra tomato seedlings in it before you use it on a larger scale. Juglone, they explain, "is tomato Kryptonite." If it don't hurt the tamatas, it won't hurt other plants.

Oh, and if you *DO* get a bad reaction from your tomato test, don't toss that black gold! Use it to feed your bluegrass lawn and/or to feed and/or mulch some of the other "insensitive" plants mentioned a minute or two ago that don't seem to be bothered by bad ol' juglone.

18 Compost Starters and Activators

A few years ago, I would probably have told you that compost activators were *totally* worthless, since various studies had found that piles to which these concentrated amounts of beneficial organisms were added at the beginning didn't become compost any faster than similar piles with no added activators. But my opinion about these products has recently been changed somewhat. Turns out they *DO* have value, but not when used according to the directions on most of the packages.

As we explained way back in the beginning of this here book, the shredded leaves that make up the bulk of your compost are already teeming with the little creatures that make compost happen. The actual composting process occurs when those microscopic creatures use your nitrogen-rich materials for food—essentially "eating" your kitchen waste and grass clippings. Now well fed, they breed like mad, generate lots of heat, and when it's all over, you've got compost.

Now, if you're backed into the corner of the leafless and have to try and make compost using straw or wood shavings or such, then, yes, by all means use an activator in the very beginning when you combine your materials—there's no life in *those* dry browns. But if you're using leaves, don't add the activator at the beginning; you've already got all the organisms you need. (But you should still toss a couple of handfuls of finished compost or garden soil into each newly made pile or filled drum. Like we said, it *may* give that pile a little microbial kick-start, but it is *certainly* good luck.)

Save your purchased "starter/activators" till the very end. New research has found that many composts *could* use a little kick *AFTER* they're finished. That's right—*after*! For much the same reason we tell you to use your compost tea right away—the clock is ticking for the living creatures in there!

Lots of beneficial creatures are killed by the heat of the composting process itself, and many others simply reach the end of their natural life span around that time. So, after a batch of compost is finished, mix the recommended amount of activator directly into the *finished* batch. Let it sit for 24 hours so the organisms can colonize the entire batch of compost, and then use it. That way, you'll be sure to be adding the maximum amount of beneficial life to your soils—and compost teas too. This would be *especially* helpful for batches of "cold" compost.

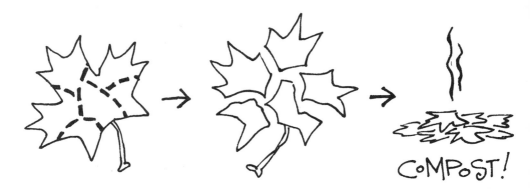

19 Troubleshooting a Bad Batch

If you're the type of person who has to measure *EVERYTHING* and frets about following directions to the letter, relax and take a deep breath. Once again—and I really can't say this enough—you have a *tremendous* amount of wiggle room when you make compost.

Yes, we toss out terms like "30-to-1 carbon-to-nitrogen ratio" and "four parts shredded leaves to each part green matter," but the truth is that these materials *WANT* to decompose—it's nature's way, after all—and you can be off by quite a bit and still make darn good compost.

If you simply remember that Fall leaves and barnyard manures can be composted alone, but green waste cannot, and that the ingredients have to be moist and stay moist, without getting *sopping* wet, you'll probably never have a problem. Yes, airflow *is* important, and turning your compost *is* great—but these things only speed the process along and make a higher-quality compost. If you don't do them, it'll just take longer; there won't be any visible or smellable problems.

And on the rare, rare occasion something *does* go wrong, and you *can* see or smell a problem, here's what to do:

If your pile, bin, or drum emits a sulfur-like (rotten egg) smell, it's likely the result of being too wet and too contained. Tear apart the pile or empty the drum, spread the material around, mix in some dry shredded leaves, let it all dry out for a bit, and then put it back—but make *sure* it gets better airflow. If it was in one of those solid plastic composters, let it sit out in the open, or put it in a wooden-slatted bin or other container with better air circulation. If it was in a drum or tumbler, check the airflow screens; I'll bet they got all clogged up and need a good cleaning. And turn that crank or tumble that spinner around more often to keep the materials mixing.

A DELIGHTFUL EARTHY AROMA WITH A HINT of MAPLE LEAF AND a NICE OAK FINISH.

If there's an ammonia smell to your compost, you've made the *VERY* common mistake of adding too much green waste to the mix. You need more dry browns in there! Remember—green waste *NEEDS* dry brown material, and lots of it; that green stuff is really just food for the creatures who are going to turn all those shredded leaves into compost for you! Mix the new brown material in well—make sure it's well-shredded!—and things should be fine.

Those are really the only two problems you're likely to encounter. A dry pile won't compost, but it won't smell bad either. A pile that's so hot it's emitting steam is simply a well-made hot compost doing what it should; remember, it can reach 160 degrees in there!

No matter what, *never* apply compost to your soil or plants that doesn't look or smell right. Only use compost that's black in color and has a distinctive, earthy smell.

Oh, and finally, if you see white steaks or a gray, powdery residue in your compost, don't worry—that's *not* a problem. In fact, it shows that your compost did indeed heat up quite a bit! That powder is what's left of likely billions of little actinomycetes (ack-tin-o-my-seats), the beneficial microbes that form in a pile when it's at its hottest. So white powder isn't a problem—it's a sign you made high quality compost.

PART 4 | Worm Bins and Store Bought: Compost from Other Sources

In which we veer into vermiculture, merge with municipal mulch, meander through mushrooms, brawl over bio-solids, peruse packaged products, get catty about chitin, sum it all up, and send you off to practice agricultural alchemy.

20 Buying Black Gold in Bulk

Yes, the purpose of this book *is* to get you making your own compost—or improving the way you do that wonderful thing, or convincing you to make seventeen times more than you already do. But sooner or later, almost all of us are going to need to step outside our own little sustainable landscape and have the occasional big honking load delivered, no matter how good you are at the Science of Rotting.

Maybe you're installing a new lawn and want to create a more fertile soil over a large area to receive the seed. Maybe you don't have enough room to make enough of your own compost to suit all your gardening needs (saw a *lot* of hands go up on *that* one…). And maybe you've just now decided to get off the chemical treadmill and want to feed your landscape naturally *while* you make your own first batches.

Good for *all* of youse!

There's no shame in buying some black gold. I personally started the garden at our current home with purchased mushroom soil (a somewhat regional product I'll discuss more in a minute), used *several* truck loads (around 23 tons each) of the same mushroom soil many years later to revitalize the lawn at our local church's centuries-old graveyard (so, *yes*—when I said earlier in the book that I knew for a personal fact that compost makes a great lawn food, I *wasn't* just whistling Z. Z. Top's "Sharp Dressed Man"), and I have a small load dropped off at my house every couple of years to play around with—if for no other reason than to be able to talk about the experience with some personal authority (as opposed to theoretically, like the worm-composting section to follow).

It is good to buy compost: You're not using chemical fertilizers, you're improving the structure of your soil, you're adding (insert voice of the late Carl Sagan here) "billions and billions of beneficial microbial creatures to that soil," and you're not using chemical fertilizers.

Oh, and you're also not using chemical fertilizers—did I mention that part yet?

But I'm no expert in how bulk composts are made and sold across this great land of ours, so I called upon a couple of someones who are: Ohio State University Professor Emeritus Harry Hoitink, Ph.D., and University of Maryland Professor Emeritus Frank Gouin, Ph.D. Both men have authored numerous technical papers and Extension Bulletins on the subject and are sought-after speakers and consultants in the composting field (despite Dr. Hoitink's endless pleas of "don't you people listen? I'm trying to retire!").

SO, WHERE DO YOU WANT IT?

COMPOST

Both have also been involved in large-scale composting operations for decades, designing huge systems for cities and industries, and helping develop testing procedures for raw ingredients and finished products. They probably know as much or more than anyone about what's going on when former waste products get transformed from trash to treasure. Here are their thoughts (via me, of course—so if it's right, they said it; if it's dumb, it's mine).

Composted Yard Waste

It's an amazing success story. People's collected grass clippings, Fall leaves, tree trimmings, and pulled weeds used to be a huge component of municipal waste streams—very expensive to landfill because of the sheer volume (often accounting for a whopping one-third of all the trash collected) and expensive to incinerate because of the high moisture content. Today, Dr. Hoitink explains, it's rare to find any of this stuff going to a landfill; it is almost all turned into compost— compost that he and Dr. Dan Herms (an Ohio State colleague, quoted along with Dr. H. back in the mulching section) feel is your #1 choice. (Dr. Gouin thinks it's great too, but he has a different #1, which we'll reveal in a minute.)

Composted yard waste, the Drs. H. explain, is essentially free of contaminants (it might be *COMPLETELY* free if you people would stop throwing those empty plastic soda bottles in with your grass clippings—they're the biggest problem!). It makes a beautiful black landscape mulch, a perfect plant food, and has very high plant-disease-fighting capabilities. Which only makes sense, after all—it's the exact same material (Fall leaves, dead plants, and tree branches) that creates "duff," the perfect natural fertilizer you find covering the forest floor. (*NOT* the beer on *The Simpsons*—although come to think of it, maybe that's what Homer's "Duff" is brewed with.)

Small communities, explains Dr. Hoitink, usually run their own yard-waste composting operations. Larger ones—like big cities—often contract it out. But just about everyone does it—there are more than 3,000 active sites processing yard waste across the country! When Fall leaves are picked up in bulk at curbside, crews will first sweep the streets (to keep road trash out of the resulting compost), collect the

Fall leaves residents have piled up (or sometimes bagged) for them, and then haul it all off to a composting facility where it will break down, generally with help from large machines that turn the piles.

In most cases, these same piles will also contain other yard waste—Spring and Fall prunings (no, you *shouldn't* prune any plants in the Fall, but people still do), pulled weeds, and grass clippings. In some (smaller) areas you have to take your yard waste to the composting site personally; in most areas it's picked up on some sort of schedule. Call your local township/municipal office to find out what your deal is.

Generally, the compost created at small-scale operations (and some larger ones) is then offered back to the local residents whose yard waste went into making it—sometimes it's given away; sometimes it's sold. And/or it could be sold to local nurseries and garden centers for use in their own plant production and/or for them to sell from big piles. Either way, you have a huge advantage here in that you can visit your compost before taking it away or buying a batch to have delivered to your home.

Yard waste composts are generally trouble-free. They should, as we've said, be the best bulk compost you can obtain. It's unlikely that somebody is trying to illegally dispose of toxic waste like old pressure-treated wood or railroad ties this way. Still, it doesn't hurt to begin the process by asking: "So—what's it made from?"

The best answers: "Just composted leaves" or "leaves and local yard waste."

The worst answer: "...and wood scraps, old pallets...."

Just say no to wood scrap composts—especially down South, where large amounts of toxic wood have turned up in landscape use after extreme hurricane damage. Rather than dispose of such wood and construction debris legally, some of it gets chipped up and dyed and sold for mulch—with horticulturally tragic results. (Yet *another* reason to avoid wood mulches!) It's hard to imagine that some of this trash doesn't find its way into local compost operations as well. Luckily, some great newspaper reporting exposed this scandal in Florida and officials have been on heightened alert ever since.

Don't get *TOO* paranoid ("Hey! Who's that behind you?!" Sorry...) but *do* be somewhat wary of *any* bulk landscape material after a large-scale house and structure-wrecking disaster in your area—especially near large bodies of water, where the prospect of toxic preserved wood use is higher.

Anyway, after you get your "original content" answer (which the first person you encounter at a garden center probably will not know—ask to speak to someone who does, like the one who purchases it), reach into the pile and pull out a handful. It should look and feel earthy, like an idealized form of soil. It should not have a sour smell, an ammonia smell, or any other disagreeable smell. It should not be dusty dry or sopping wet.

Don't worry if you don't feel overly confident here. That's natural. But the truth is that you'll do just fine. Your nose should be able to detect "off" smells as well as anyone's—and Dr. Hoitink feels that the human nose is *very* attuned to the pleasant smell good compost will have; he says it's the same smell you pick up on a relaxing Spring or Fall walk through the forest.

This inspection process, as he puts it, is a lot like the "duck" test: "If it looks like good compost, smells like good compost, and feels like good compost, then it probably *IS* good compost."

A final note here: If you *can* get good compost for free at a local yard-waste composting site, you'll almost certainly have to haul it away yourself. If you don't have access to a pickup (or ideally, larger) truck or have a lot of experience hauling bulky, heavy loads, hire someone to do it. The township may do it for a fee, or the workers at the site may provide such a service on the side if you ask.

Of course, you'll have to pay for your compost at a local nursery or garden center—but nine times out of ten, they'll have a delivery system in place. If you're the type who hates to pay shipping for anything, go ahead and try and haul it yourself (perhaps racking up a couple of grand in doctor and chiropractor bills to save a fifty-buck delivery fee). If, however, you're more like me and no longer go out of your way to seek out heavy, dirty work, pay for the delivery—it will be well worth it.

Mushroom Soil

My familiarity with this product turns out to be a function of where I live: Southeastern Pennsylvania, home to the largest concentration of mushroom farms in the U.S.—and the planet.

There are *many* large-to-huge-scale growing operations centered around Kennett Square, Pennsylvania ("the mushroom capital of the world!"), and a smaller but still significant number near Reading, PA. These operations typically fill their huge indoor growing systems with a very rich mixture of organic matter. The farm I'm most familiar with uses a combination of fresh horse manure, "spoiled" straw (sat out in the field too long, got wet before harvest, or some other non-toxic thing happened that made it unsellable the regular way), and ground-up corncobs. Some other mushroom growers prefer poultry for the manure

portion of the equation; some use a mix of manures. Others (especially growers of specialty mushrooms that require very specific growing mediums) use very different mixes—but it all tends to look pretty much the same on the back end.

Typically, they grow a few runs of mushrooms in this fresh, black, hot, and steamy stuff and then, when the 'shrooms start to decrease in size, move it all out and bring fresh "soil" in. And "a few" really *is* only two or three runs.

As you can imagine, this means there's a *huge* amount of organic matter being generated that needs somewhere to go. This material can be called (among other synonyms): mushroom soil, spent mushroom soil, mushroom compost, spent mushroom compost, and sometimes just plain compost. One thing it is *NOT* is "spent"—it's teeming with nutrients. The material I use, from a distributor by the name of Hawk Valley Farms (they handle the soil from a farm that steams their product at the end to kill all the mushroom spores that would otherwise keep germinating—some other farms use formaldehyde), tests out at a very nice 2-2-3 on the NPK scale, and is almost impossibly high in organic matter—the test reports I'm looking at now say the organic matter content is an astounding 69 percent! *And* it's never been used to grow a *green plant*—only fungi, so your plants will get plenty of good eating (and great disease prevention).

Put a pin in a map where Delaware, Maryland, and Pennsylvania meet. That's where you'll find the big guys. The closer you are to that latitude and longitude (or that of Reading, which is located a little deeper into Pennsylvania), the more likely you are to find big piles of the stuff for sale at garden centers or available for delivery. (Although some non-local nurseries like it so much they truck it all the way to places like Ohio and the Great Lakes.)

The closer you are, the less expensive it will be, as delivery can often cost more than the material itself. But don't look at that as a negative—this differential largely reflects the *very* low price the compost itself is usually sold for, plus the fact that fuel *IS* expensive and the big trucks necessary (like the 26-foot-long dumper plus a ten-foot-long cab that carries the really big batches for Hawk Valley) don't get real good mileage. Bottom line: You'll still be getting a huge amount of very rich material for a very low price.

Typically, you can buy it two ways: Fresh or aged.

"Fresh" mushroom soil is just what it sounds like—*fresh* out of the mushroom houses. It has a strong smell of manure and is surprisingly hot. (Experienced gardeners can use it to play wonderful horticultural tricks like creating a "French hot bed" cold frame that will grow beautiful salad greens in the dead of a Northern Winter. *Really* handy folks could run some pipes and use the center of a huge pile to heat water over Winter.)

Although the sellers call it "compost," our pal Dr. Hoitink would likely pronounce it "incomplete" or "immature." Or maybe he was just talking about me. Anyway, fresh is the cheapest—you can often get a huge truckload (like Hawk Valley's 36-foot-long tractor trailer) delivered for about the same price as a *much* smaller load of "aged." If you have the room and the time, have it dropped off, let it cook down for six to nine months (six or less in warm weather; closer to nine in cool to cold climes), and it will *become* aged. (Dr. Gouin estimates it will shrink in size by about one-third during this time.) Many garden centers or nurseries have big fresh batches dropped off in the Fall that they let age and sell in bulk in the Spring.

However, most regular people don't have that kind of room—or the necessary expertise to know when to use this rapidly changing material safely—so they buy "aged," fresh mushroom soil that's sat in big piles, hopefully being turned occasionally, for that six or nine months. Such material should pass what we will now call the quack test (mostly to embarrass Dr. H): Give it a feel and a sniff. It may have a light, lingering smell of manure and be *slightly* warmer than homemade compost, but nothing *too* strong or at all hot. (If it is either, let it sit awhile.)

Dr. Gouin concurs that a quack test is essential for any purchased (or even home-made) compost. He says to look for a rich, earthy smell, dark color, small particle size, and moisture in the 45-50 percent range (like a sponge that's been wrung out and is still moist, but not wet), and very few—if any—recognizable original ingredients.

Obviously, if it's sitting outside someplace for sale, you can pick some up and see if it quacks to your satisfaction. If, however, you're ordering a load to be delivered blind, you should only purchase from someone a friend or neighbor has had a good experience with, and/or who can supply recent test results that show it meets all the requirements of nutrition and safety (no detectable herbicides, fungicides, or other horticultural chemicals) and has a low salt content (this will likely be indicated as something like "E/C" or "total conductivity"; you want those numbers to be 6 to 8 percent or less).

If at all possible, tool on down to the yard for a visit beforehand. Ideally, you should also plan to be home when it's delivered so you can inspect the load *before* it gets dumped onto your driveway. (*That's* a genie that would be *DARN* hard to put back in the bottle!) Don't make this a surprise inspection—tell them you'll want to check it on site. (This may also motivate them to bring the *REALLY* good stuff.)

Dr. Hoitink adds that mushroom compost should be applied in the Fall if you have clay soils and in the Spring if you have sandy soil. If the manure used in its original production *has* made it a little salty, this will allow the salt to be washed out. Dr. Gouin heartily agrees. If you're using it to feed your garden soil, everyone says to till it in. If you wish to use it as a decorative or disease-suppressing mulch, go right ahead— just make sure there's *no* heat left to the touch, warns Dr. Gouin.

And, of course, go slowly—it's always easier to add a little more than to try and hurriedly remove a whole lot if your plants start to seem stressed.

I should add here that I didn't know *ANY* of this when I bought my first batch, did everything wrong, and didn't lose a single plant.

We had bought a house in the woods (which should tell you quite a bit about how gardening-savvy I was. Snow White had moved out because there wasn't enough sun for her flowers [although she *did* say she was going to miss the dish-washing birds and chipmunks]), and the earth in the only area I could clear for a potential garden was comprised of a *VERY* thin layer of topsoil (OK—it was clay; what are you, a cop?) over what appeared to be the ruins of Atlantis.

Luckily, a neighbor with a fine garden explained that he amended his soil yearly from a big pile of rich, black earth sitting off to one side of where we were talking. "Mushroom soil," he explained, purchased fresh from Hawk Valley several years ago. The pile was still huge. He offered me a batch, and I accepted.

So we spent the better part of a day filling a pickup bed full to the top, driving the half-mile to my place and then shoveling it all out onto my garden-to-be. Once spread out, this massive load covered my thousand square feet with a layer easily as thick as a facial tissue. "I need my own load," I wisely decided.

I should have known I was in trouble when the neighborhood children came by on their bikes to watch the massive truck dump its load. Apparently my math skills were as poor as my old high school grades indicated, and I had *slightly* miscalculated how deeply sixteen tons of mushroom soil would cover my thousand square feet. (Their trucks were loaded differently, and so the batches were significantly lighter back then—thank God!)

I did not come to this conclusion immediately. No, I first had to wander through the stages of fear, denial, anger, grief, etc.

It was only after deciding, "it just needs to be spread out more evenly" and climbing to the top of the pile with a shovel that I realized two things that towed my attitude inexorably toward acceptance.

1. I was now looking into our second floor bedroom window.

2. My ankles were getting *hot*!

So I put an ad in the "Swap Shop" at work, inviting people to come by and fill up their pickups for $10 a load. Lots of gardeners at work, so I got lots of takers—fifteen in the first few days. That put me $50 ahead on the money end (the load had cost just shy of a hundred bucks—delivered; but gas was a lot cheaper back then). On "the steaming black mound the size of a large mobile home sitting atop what I had once hoped would be a garden" end, however, things were unchanged. They hadn't made a perceivable dent.

So I shoveled tons down the side of the gulley I was lucky enough to have next to the garden spot, created growing beds everywhere on the property, sold more, gave some away, and finally got it down to about a foot-high layer, which, after a few weeks of just mixing it all up, I was *finally* able to till into the soil.

By all accounts, it was still *way* too much. By all accounts, it was still *way* too fresh.

But I had a pretty good garden that year. And an even better one the year after.

Would I do it again?

Yes, if I were in the same situation of starting from scratch—and had a big enough area to merit The Big Boy order. *And* if I were that age (or younger).

Otherwise, no. My taste for adventure has dimmed with my advancing realization that trouble knows how to find me well enough without my going out looking for it. But two truckloads of the same stuff (*VERY* fresh, and much heavier with their new loading system) is what we used recently (the Falls of 2003 and 2004—we did it in stages so as not to crush our volunteers) to revitalize that lawn at my church's ancient cemetery—with astoundingly positive results.

I would certainly recommend a big, honkin' fresh load to anyone who had a lot of land and a big paved area (or grassy spot they wished to smother anyway) on which to store it, and some basic knowledge of gardening or composting. And a big honkin' load of *aged* to anyone with the room and the need.

And I will personally continue to get much smaller loads of aged mushroom soil (Hawk Valley recently bought a baby truck just for pikers like me) every once and again. I just love the stuff.

"Bio-Solids"—i.e. Composted Human Waste

This is a *very* controversial subject, and one that people squeamish about such things may want to skip—with the warning that it is an important subject, that more cities are offering compost generated by their waste treatment plants all the time, and that anyone who buys compost in bulk should know the right questions to ask about such material. And don't assume you know *EXACTLY* what goes into such material if you don't read further.

(And let's be honest; we're all "contributing" to the component of this material that you WERE just thinking of—unless angels come and take yours away in the middle of the night.)

Anyway, that said, "this"—composted human waste—is Dr. Gouin's #1 choice for purchased compost.

Much of this kind of compost goes directly into the business of agriculture and horticulture, but sometimes it is available to homeowners. Compost made utilizing a city's sewage must be analyzed on a constant basis—any contaminants and salt levels must be below prescribed (EPA) levels, and there must be a paper trail to prove it. So folks in a position to buy these composts have an excellent idea of just what they're getting.

In discussing his fondness for such composts, Dr. Gouin related that none other than Frank Rizzo—the legendary mayor of my hometown, Philadelphia, in the 60s and 70s (you may recall a famous photo of the former chief of police; told while attending a formal dinner that a riot had broken out, he appeared at the scene with a nightstand tucked into his cummerbund)—was an early pioneer of what I'll call the "clean pipe" system. He very much wanted to cut the city's sewage sludge disposal costs, and perhaps realized that there was tremendous agricultural potential in the massive amounts of the stuff they were then consigning to landfills and dumping in the ocean.

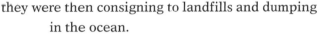

THE ORIGINAL" COMPOSTER.

Dr. Gouin explained to "The Mayor" that, although the very topic makes some people squirm, composted human waste is an excellent fertilizer. "Night soil" (perhaps the perfect euphemism) was used to feed the soil and protect the Chinese people from famine for untold centuries; and proper composting, he explained, makes it perfectly safe for people to handle.

The problem, as he explained to Big Frank back then, is that small-scale idiots pour stuff like used motor oil down the drain and large-scale criminals use sewers for illegal disposal of their toxic industrial waste. So The Mayor did two things. First, he had a system set in place that diverted the sewage from residential districts to a composting operation. Second, he put industries in or near those areas on notice that the city would be checking for pollutants in their wastewater. The result was a material that experts like Dr. Gouin and "Compost Science & Utilization" publisher Jerry Goldstein (more on him in a minute) say they would not hesitate to use or recommend.

Dr. Gouin adds that many cities now follow this model, some selling the result under localized brand names—like "Orgro" in the Baltimore area. (The famous Milorganite brand, however, is not one of these; this Milwaukee-based product is made from *dried* waste. It is not composted, and therefore it was not recommended by anyone I spoke with.)

All bio-solids must be identified as such, and information sheets and test results must be available to consumers. So, to misquote the wonderful 60's comedy group The Firesign Theatre, if you weren't one of the squirmers a few graphs back, you may decide that "it's really *GOOD* compost, Mrs. Preskie!"

I have the greatest respect for the opinions of both Dr. Gouin and Jerry Goldstein, who heartily endorse it. (I didn't discuss it much with Dr. Hoitink—he's more of a yard waste expert, while Dr. Gouin has more bio-solid experience.) It is, however, *NOT* allowed for use in organic agriculture. And there are recent revelations (literally as we go to press) about antibiotics and other pharmaceuticals surviving the composting process and being detected in the finished stuff. So I personally will not recommend it—other than to say that if it's your only choice besides chemicals, I might turn my head.

That's the basics on purchased composts—I could go into much more detail, but most of it would not be applicable to the folks I'm writing this for. In other words, if you're in charge of a farm, huge landscaping or greenhousing operation, golf course, community garden, or other venture in which you'll be using tons a week, this book ain't gonna do it, cheapskate!

Subscribe to Jerry Goldstein's fine technical publications "BioCycle" and "Compost Utilization and Science" (they're published by his company, "JG Press") or take some classes and/or go to a couple of conferences—this stuff is big business and there's lots of great info out there. We're just feeding tamatas in the backyard here.

Other Composts

Everyone is composting waste these days, Dr. Hoitink explains:

- Food wastes captured "pre-consumer" are some of the best—the vegetable and grain wastes from food processing plants make a great raw material for composting, as do "local specialties," like grape waste from wineries and grain waste from breweries.

- Food wastes "post-consumer" (*i.e.*, leftovers) from restaurants, hospitals, nursing homes, colleges, and anyplace else that achieves critical leftover mass, *can* be composted, but you have to be careful that the result isn't too salty. You *MUST* see analyses of these composts before you use them on any large scale. On a more personal note, you may even want to think twice about composting your *own* leftovers if you're the type of person who likes your salt with a little baked potato on it.

- As we just mentioned, cities are taking the best of their sewage (diverting waste from industrial districts elsewhere and working only with the mostly "humanure" they receive from the suburbs) and composting it into "bio-solids" (which, you have to admit, sounds a whole lot better than some of the potential brand names you were thinking of).

- And some facilities do it all, mixing up food wastes, yard wastes, maybe the odd bio-solid, and composting it all down.

To say this is a complex topic is like saying the Yankees have a fairly high payroll.

Now, if you're on a college campus or some other flaming pinko, hippie-dippie place where they're composting food waste and such—congratulations! Take me with you! (I miss college!!) Sorry—anyway, if you are in a place where they process a lot of leftovers into community compost, make sure it looks and smells OK *and* that the salt content gets checked. They use a lot of salt to cook the stuff to begin with, and most Americans seem to shake first and ask questions later.

The Bottom Line

* Drs. Hoitink and Herms choose locally produced yard waste compost for their #1. No one I spoke with had any negative feelings about it.

* I agree, with a nudge toward well-aged mushroom composts, which Dr. Gouin likes a lot, and Dr. Hoitink has some slight reservations about.

* And Dr. Gouin and compost expert Jerry Goldstein rave about well-documented bio-solids, which make great use of an excellent raw material, but can't be used by people who wish to be certified organic (or who choose to grow just like the certified crowd). And there are those presciption drug residues to consider.

Almost every area in the nation has the first type available. I'm guessing that—objectively—it really is the best possible kind. And you don't have much—if anything—to worry about or check; just give it the quack test and go home early.

I just adore my mushroom soil, and expect it will make you very happy, if a high-quality version is available in your area. But some people don't like it—especially people who live near the farms and are overwhelmed by the pungent aroma of untold tons at times.

I came into this discussion somewhat suspicious of bio-solids (maybe I have a little "squirm" in me), but I have tremendous respect for the experts who endorse it. The great Jerry Goldstein—himself a much-admired former editor-in-chief of *Organic Gardening* magazine—has been lobbying me on behalf of bio-solids for many, many years. Luckily for me, I can cite the organic prohibition and pharmaceutical hangover concern or this 'graph might go on for fourteen more pages. If I were running a golf course in an area where it was avaiable and wanted to get my lawn off drugs, I'd certainly give a batch the quack test.

Compost in a Bag

I thought I was going to get away without having to talk about this, but my editor just yanked me back. Ouch.

If we're talking about the cheap, wet, heavy, generically bagged stuff without a lot of info on the label, it is not my first choice. (Or second, or third, or....) It is not anyone's choice, really. The labels and names on these things are generally somewhere between darn confusing and extremely misleading. And whatever kind of "compost" is in that bag, it's been sealed in there without air for a long time. So *AT BEST* it might be an "OK" compost that can provide some plant food, but none of the disease-fighting life we compost-users depend upon for a happy, healthy garden.

If it's all you can find, Drs. Herms and Gouin and myself all independently came to the same conclusion: Buy a single, sample bag, take it home, open it up, and give it the "quack" test. If it seems OK, go back and get more. Dr. Herms suggests you then empty the bags out all together, mix them up (maybe with a little *REAL* compost) and let it all sit for a while. (For good luck—OK?) Maybe add one of those "compost starter/activators" to bring a little life to the party.

Now, this dissing does NOT apply to *high-quality* premium bagged composts, like the "Coast of Maine" brand I've been seeing locally (Pennsylvania and the Washington, DC, area) in better garden centers and natural food stores. Dr. Gouin really likes two similar products produced in the Baltimore area: "Chesapeake Blue" (crab wastes composted with sawdust) and "Chesapeake Green" (composted poultry "litter"—another way of referring to a combination of manure and bedding). Both are nicely rich in nitrogen (you may remember me recommending those two raw ingredients for super-charged compost pile heating back in the beginning of this book), and Chesapeake Blue has the added advantage of being rich in *chitin* (pronounced "kite-in"), a substance that occurs naturally in seafood shells, survives the composting process, and makes the soil it's applied to toxic to destructive nematodes. In the North, these creatures generally only attack a few ornamentals, specifically boxwoods. But down South (again, as we mentioned back in the do-it-yourself section), root knot nematodes are a destructive, aggravating, and frustrating pest that plagues vegetable gardens. Search for chitin-rich composts, my Southern friends, and you will be happy.

Some other high-quality bagged composts are available from organically oriented mail order supply companies, like the "Gardener's Gold Compost" sold by *Gardens Alive!* and "Vermont Compost Plus" from *Johnny's Selected Seeds.*

And that's just the few brands I'm familiar with. There are probably hundreds of such products available across the country— these things tend to be regionally produced and packaged. But you will likely know them when you see them, just as you would good compost. They will cost a little more, have a lot more info on the label, and basically give you a warm and fuzzy feeling all over.

There are also what I'll call specialty composts; for instance, I would consider things like bagged worm castings, composted llama poop, and the various "Zoo Doos" (composted rhino and elephant leavings) to fit into this category.

Although they'd be much too expensive to use on a large scale, I wouldn't hesitate to buy a few bags to freshen up a porch full of house plants, protect a prized rose bush or two from dread disease, or other small-scale use.

The stuff I'm talking about *avoiding* is the big, wet, heavy plastic bag with very little labeling selling for a buck or two at the big box stores, like Home Depot and Lowe's. That's "fill," not "food."

Oh, and one final note (hey—my editor just keeled over laughing; I wonder why), peat moss is *NOT* compost. It is a great natural product that lowers soil *pH*, is an essential component in seed-starting and potting mixes, and a natural antibiotic that prevents damping-off and some other diseases. But it is too light in weight for many applications, contains little or no actual nutrition, and can radically lower the *pH* of

some soils whether you want it to or not. Now don't get me wrong: I like peat moss. I use peat moss. Peat moss is a friend of mine. But I know compost, and peat moss is *NOT* compost.

One *OTHER* final note (oh—*THAT'S* why my editor was laughing), Dr. Gouin wants to make clear that dried or dehydrated products (like Milorganite and dehydrated cow manure) are *not* compost. As you should certainly have picked up by now, composting is a complex process by which raw ingredients are changed by living organisms and processes. Drying is not the same—not even close. Dried something-or-other might make an OK fertilizer, but it won't do all the wonderful things that living compost does.

Now I'm really done. Ah-HEM: "Hey, Editor—you can stop laughing now, OK???!"

21 Vermiculture—Making Compost with Worms

What if you live in an apartment or tiny house with no room to compost outside, but you still have a green thumb? Maybe you've got a balcony overflowing with pots. Or lots of houseplants in a big window. Or a house with a postage-stamp-size lawn and teeennny tiny garden area outside. *AND* you really like the basic idea of recycling your coffee grounds, eggshells, lettuce leaves, and the like into primo fertilizer for your bonsai life.

You, my friend, need woims. But not just any woims. No—you need Red Wrigglers, ♪ "the Cadillac of worms" ♪ . (*Eisenia fetida,* to you science buffs out there.)

Seriously, worm composting—or vermiculture as the experts call it (a term I hate—it sounds like you're taking rats to the opera)—*DOES* create super-duper, double-secret-probation premium compost. I am loathe to admit it, but the distinctively lumpy compost (technically "castings") produced by these helpful little creatures is actually better in some ways than the best home-made or yard-waste composts.

Something amazing happens to food and soil as it travels through the gut of a worm. Somehow, the stuff that comes out the other end is super-charged, literally *rippling* with nutrients and trace elements. You almost have to be careful—worm castings are *SO* nutritious that a little goes a long, long way. (Which is good, because home-scale operations don't produce huge amounts.)

To begin, you need a container with air holes (screened, to keep the compost—and worms—from spilling out). Size? How much room've you got? Some people get by with something the size of a five-gallon bucket under the sink. But bigger is better, of course—most of the indoor ones I see are the size of a medium-large Rubbermaid storage container (of course, maybe that's because most of the indoor ones I see *ARE* medium-large Rubbermaid storage containers).

People with more room should have bigger bins—the size of the bin determines the amount of kitchen garbage you can process. If you want to recycle lots—say from a family of four that actually cooks some meals at home (what a quaint idea!)—you want a big bin, maybe down in the basement or out in an insulated or heated garage.

First, you put some "bedding" in. Typically people use shredded black-and-white newspaper pages, which work great—but I have to wonder what kind of amazing stuff you'd create if the bedding were a more natural material, like shredded Fall leaves. Anyway, you mix in some kitchen garbage and then add the worms—which yes, really are called Red Wrigglers, a bait worm of choice that is also available mail-

order from suppliers of—well, vermicomposting supplies (duh). And, no, regular old earthworms won't work.

Besides, you should only need to buy worms once. After that you've got your own perpetual motion machine happening down there. The worms will process the bin's contents, because that's what worms do. You keep an eye on things, and when it looks done (you'll know), you move it all over to one side and place fresh bedding and garbage on the other. The worms will naturally move over to the new raw materials, and after they do, you harvest the finished product and add some more raw stuff to make up the difference. You shouldn't have any worms in the finished compost to deal with. If you find one moping around, name it "Gilligan" and toss it back.

And so on and so on....

Is it really all that simple? Like outdoor composting, yes and no. The worms need a certain amount of warmth—these bins can't be kept outdoors in cold weather in most parts of the country, because if the poor little wormies freeze, "they're dead, Jim." ("I can't help them, Spock; I'm a *DOCTOR*—not a vermicologist!")

It is also a good idea to have a little spigot in the bottom of the bin to drain off the liquid that tends to accumulate when a lot of the raw materials are very wet (and, yes—this worm juice IS essentially super-duper compost tea; I would advise thinning it out to the color of weak tea before feeding your plants with it. But I would absolutely advise thinning it out and feeding your plants with it. And save some for me!*).

If you provide the correct conditions, the worms will be fruitful and multiply, and you'll need to thin the herd occasionally. Toss them into your garden, other people's gardens, give them to fishermen—excuse me, fisher*people*—or to folks looking to start their own bin; and, of course, save one to put in the hair of the kid who sits in front of you in Western Civ class.

(* My *plants*, that is.)

As I explained/admitted earlier, this is not something I have ever done personally. I've never even worm-sat. But I have visited many classrooms where a big wooden bin full o' worms was a wonderful center of attention (and constant food provider for parents' and teachers' houseplants), and I recommend them highly in such situations—kids love them, they are wonderfully instructive, and you have something alive in the classroom that doesn't make people sneeze or need to be walked. *And* whose poop is a plus instead of a problem— take *that*, Fido!

If I lived in an apartment, I would *NEED* one, whether I was a gardener or not, as I am incapable of throwing broccoli stalks and lettuce leaves away without massive pangs of guilt, regret, and remorse. And nicely packaged castings make a great gift for gardeners. Really! C'mon, guys—anybody can buy her a dozen roses. Only *YOU* can give her a box (get a really fancy one from a store like Tiffany's) filled with rich, black, worm poop!

If you'd like to give worm ranching a try, I heartily endorse it. Part compost making, part solid waste recycling, and part easy-care pet ownership, worm wrangling is fun *and* productive—try and get that out of your Amazing Sea Monkeys!

If you *ARE* going to try this, please read up a bit on it first. There are many good sources of information out there—including online articles (be sure to check out "worm woman dot com," the site of the late, great vermicologist, Mary Applehof), bulletins available from your local extension service agents and Master Gardeners, and more.

And ask around to see if anyone nearby already has a system going—they'll be a great source of advice, encouragement, and quite likely, some worms.

Check out stores and web sites and you'll see a huge variety of bins for sale—including really classy ones designed to resemble fine furniture. You'll also find several different "tower" style bins; these are made of stackable sections, with multiple levels that the worms can move in and out of for easier filling and harvesting. And, of course, regular-looking small ones, big ones, wood ones, plastic ones...

If you're handy, go ahead and make one. There are lots of directions available on the Internet and in books. If you're more like me ("Oops!" *Crash*! "Oh—ha, ha—nothing, honey—nothing at all. But I'll be down here for a little while longer than I thought. Oh, and how late is the hospital open?"), do a little research, find a style that suits your needs with the air holes all there and the spigot all in place nicely sealed, and buy it.

And if it's the *ONLY* way you can make compost, please do it.

✳ Final Thoughts

This book is both too long and too short—too simple and too complex. I have probably made the easy seem too difficult. And I'm sure I've oversimplified far too many complex things.

The simple truth is that—despite the act of composting itself being a very specific natural phenomenon—no two people familiar with the topic are ever going to describe it the same way. Most others would have gone into a lot more scientific detail and footnoting, talking ceaselessly about things like "recalcitrant materials" and carbon-to-nitrogen ratios and naming in mind-boggling Latin all the diseases that compost has been shown to combat.

Some others would have described the process much more simply than I have. There is a lot of truth in saying we could just have printed up a big banner that says, "pile it up and it will rot" and covered the topic quite well, thank you very much.

Could I have gone into a lot more detail about vermiculture? You bet. But that wasn't my goal in getting into this ring, so be thankful you got what you did.

Could I have completely avoided the section on buying compost? You bet. But that would not have worked toward my personal goal of helping as many of you as possible get your landscape off toxins and onto a healthy, balanced diet.

Could I have gone into more detail about composting in arid regions or what to do in really cold areas where your compost freezes for nine months of the year and then you have poor sledding? You bet. But that kind of information is better gleaned locally.

What I think we *have* done here is provide enough info for a good 95 percent of you to proceed to compost correctly—or buy really good stuff. I would have killed for a 95 back in high school, and will be real happy with it now. (All right; all right—*85*; but that's the last crack I want to hear from you!)

Because now it's time to make like Nike, to make like Mikey (this one, not the kid who wouldn't eat anything—I *wish* that were MY problem!)...

...and just go do it.

Get started. Try. Fail. Succeed. Excel. No book in the world is ever going to be able to prepare you for every circumstance you'll face. But none of those circumstances should be able to stop you, either. Pile it up and it *WILL* rot.

Questions?

First, call your local county extension office. They're in the phone book (do they still *MAKE* phone books??) or do a quick Internet search: Type in "Extension" and your state; the main office website (always associated with a big university) will likely be the first hit. If not, try variations of their full name: "County cooperative agricultural extension service" and your state. (Now you see why I just said "extension?")

The extension agents—and their fabulous Master Gardener helper/volunteers—are becoming more and more knowledgeable and enthusiastic about this subject. They can offer advice and printed materials—and many now run composting classes, often with a free or discounted composter available to graduates at the end.

Check out the website for my Public Radio show—"You Bet Your Garden" (dot org, net, *OR* com—I didn't take no chances!) for my other writings on compost. Shoot me an e-mail via my show's site if you have a question I haven't covered here or there—maybe you'll have it answered on the air! Whoop-dee-do!

Other gardeners who are already composting may be your absolute *best* source of advice—as with specific varieties of plants, they're down on what your local conditions mean to the operation. And they're *DOING* it.

If you search online, look for advice from university extension services; it's generally going to be the most reliable. But read everything you want. You're going to come across a lot of dissention, contradiction, and the occasional "just plain wrong" thing.

That's composting, honey. It ain't no one thing. It is alive and constantly changing, different for everyone and yet, remarkably the same, as well. There's nothing else like it. And once you start, you will never stop.

Because you will have attained the power of The Alchemist. You will have found The Sorcerer's Stone. You will know how to transform trash into treasure, lead into gold, coffee grounds into cantaloupe food.

Now get out there and make something rot. And think of me when you do.

Index

Kitchen scraps, 6, 12, 13, 14-17, 69, 70, 75, 83, 109
Kudzu, 73
Landfill, 92
Lawn, 4, 5, 41-47, 90
Lawn clippings, 6, 12, 13
Lawnmower, 9, 11, 41, 42, 77
Leaves, 3, 5, 24, 33, 39, 83, 85
    alternatives, 74-79
    blowers, 6-8
    mold, 9, 22
    shredders, 9, 77
    whole vs. shredded, 6
Leftovers, 5
Lehigh-style wooden bin, 20, 22, 25
Lettuce, 108, 111
Lilacs, 32, 36, 53
Liming recommendation, 72
Liquid fertilizers, 52, 58
Llama leavings, 17, 106
Lobster shells, 16, 23
Luck, 17, 83, 105
Manure, 69, 70, 97
Martian Manhunter, The, 54
Maryland, 96
Master Gardeners, 111, 114
Math, 11
Meat, 16
Microbes, 11
Milorganite, 102, 107
Milwaukee, 102
Minerals, 8
Miracle-Gro, 4
Moisture, 25
Moisture meter, 26
Mold, 58
Moule de feuille, 9
Moule horticole, le, 9
Mulch, 4, 37, 38, 39, 42, 43, 54, 98
Mulching mower, 13, 42
Mulching ratio, 7-8
Mushrooms/soil, 89, 90, 95-100, 104
Nature, imitating, 4, 5
Neff, Ed, 61
New England, 66
Newspaper, shredded, 79
New York Yankees, 103
"Night soil," 101
Nirvana, leaf, 9
Nitrogen, 6, 8, 10, 11, 12, 14, 16, 17, 23, 42, 49, 61, 68, 69, 70, 74, 78, 83, 105
Nitrogen immobilization, 49
North, 33, 37, 63, 73, 97, 106
Northern grass, 12, 41, 44, 46

Nutrients, 8
Ohio, 96
Ohio State University, 48, 51, 81, 91, 92
Open piles, 25
Organic fertilizer, 65, 66
Organic Gardening magazine, 1, 104
Organic matter, 6
"Orgro," 102
Osmocote, 4
Overfed soil/plants, 5, 39, 52
Oxygen, 20
Oxygenated compost tea, 60
Paper, 79
Peat moss, 32, 40, 106
Pennsylvania, 25, 46, 95, 96, 105
Pentachlorophenol, 71
Peppers, 58, 81
Perennials, 37, 78
Perlite, 32
Pesticide, 5
Pests, 9
Petunias, 81
pH, 39, 40, 49, 54, 72-73, 106-107
Philadelphia, 23
Phoenix, 46
Pitchfork, 22
Pit composting, 26
Plant-disease preventer, 4
Pond plants, 66
"Poop," dog and cat, 17, 111
Potassium, 72
Potatoes, 81
Potting mixture, 31, 32
Poultry manure, 17, 70-71, 95, 105
Powdery mildew, 58
Pre-emergent herbicide, 46
Premium triple-shredded bark, 4
Pressure-treated wood, 71, 93
Pruning, 37, 54, 93
Public Radio, national, 1, 114
Quack test, 97, 98, 104, 105
Raccoons, 16
Railroad ties, 71, 93
Rain, 25, 44, 73
Reading, Pennsylvania, 95, 96
Reasons to compost, 3-27
Recycling, 14
"Red-bag material," 37
"Red Wrigglers," 108, 109
Rhino leavings, 17, 106
Rhododendrons, 39, 40, 72, 81
Rizzo, Frank, 101, 102
Rodale, J. I., 20, 66
Rodents, 50

 # About the Author

M ike McGrath *is host of the nationally syndicated Public Radio show*
You Bet Your Garden; *garden editor for WTOP News radio in*
Washington, DC; answerer of the "Question of the Week" at the Gardens
Alive! *website; columnist and contributing editor for* GreenPrints
magazine *("The Weeder's Digest"); winner of four consecutive "Best of*
Show" awards at the Philadelphia Flower Show; former editor-in-chief of
Organic Gardening *magazine, former garden expert for the Saturday*
morning edition of The Today Show *on NBC-TV…*

…and most important, proud maker of black gold since 1985